ONE

QUESTION

*I press on toward the goal to win the prize for which
God has called me heavenward in Christ Jesus.*
PHILIPPIANS 3:14

ONE QUESTION

LIFE-CHANGING ANSWERS
FROM TODAY'S LEADING VOICES

KEN COLEMAN

RAMSEY
PRESS

To my best friend and the love of my life, Stacy:
I am forever thankful you said "Yes!" to the biggest question
I have ever asked.

And to our little ones, Ty, Chase, and Josie:
may your ceaseless questions never end.

Contents

SURVIVING

SUSTAINING

Acknowledgments

I did not plan to write this book, it just happened. There are so many people who have shaped my journey, yet words do not exist to adequately share my appreciation.

My deepest gratitude goes to my wife and soul mate, Stacy. Thank you for your unconditional love and grace. I simply would not have had the courage to pursue this opportunity without your belief and support throughout the process. You make me better each day, and I'm immeasurably blessed to share this life with you.

To our precious little ones, Ty, Chase, and Josie: you inspire me every day to ask the right questions so I can pour my heart and soul into each of your lives. Thank you for being so patient when Daddy had to work on this book. I hope that one day it marks you as much as it has me.

To my family. Mom, you nurtured me and my strengths as a child. You unflinchingly supported every leap I ever made as a young adult, no matter the odds. Dad, you stoked the fires of calling and passion early on and opened my eyes to history and my opportunity to make it. Jamie, you are a rock whose tremendous talent always pushed your big brother. Nanny, your strength inspires me every day, and your love never wavers. Todd, you are my corner man, and I cannot count the times I have had to borrow your belief in me when I was doubting. Bob and Donna, your constant affirmation and encouragement are a shot of adrenaline. I cannot thank my family and not mention my grandaddy E. H. Coleman. I must believe he can read this from Heaven. You are my hero and greatest inspiration. You were the kindest man I ever met.

You modeled a love for life and people that I desire to pass on to my children.

Thanks to Jonathan Merritt for your invaluable contributions to this book. You pushed, pulled, corrected, and celebrated the vision for this book. Working with you has been one of the most rewarding experiences of my life.

Thanks to the team at Howard—especially Jonathan Merkh, Becky Nesbitt, Holly Halverson, and Jessica Wong. Jonathan and Becky, you inspired me with your belief and vision. I am forever grateful for the opportunity to work with you both.

Thanks to Shannon Marven for taking a chance on me and working to make this book a reality.

To my friends who cheered me on and gave well-timed "atta boy"s: Jay and Landia Hassell, Bill Hampton, Gabe Lyons, Jason Locy, Brad Lomenick, Darren Whitehead, Tim Willard, Dean Parker, Jeremy Breland, Jon Acuff, Mike Gurley.

To the teachers and coaches who had a special impact on my development: Joy Bryant, Benny Polk, Jay Jarvis, Keith Hall.

To my mentors, who have selflessly given me their time, talents, and wisdom: Don Sapaugh, George Sweet, Tim Phillips.

Thanks to those of you who have taken care of me, taught me, said "yes" to me, given me an opportunity, and given me another chance. Thanks to the many people who have prayed for me over the years and continue to do so.

Finally, I stand amazed at the faithfulness of God and the marvelous things He has done.

Foreword

BY DAVE RAMSEY

When I was growing up, both of my parents were real estate professionals. They were always listening to motivational and sales training tapes in the car, so little Dave in the backseat got master's-level education in sales and leadership by the age of nine! As I got older, into my teens, Dad would occasionally hand me a book and expect me to read it, understand it, and apply it to my life. One of the best books he ever gave me was Dale Carnegie's classic *How to Win Friends and Influence People*. That book is filled with all kinds of gems, but the one that has always stood out to me most is the observation that successful people know how to engage other people in a conversation.

See, Carnegie found what we all know to be true: people like the sound of their own voices. They like to hear their names said aloud. That's true of all of us, isn't it? My wife, Sharon, and I often come away from business or social gatherings blown away by how much people like to talk about themselves. Instead of asking about you, they talk about themselves. They fill your ear with every detail about their life, their house, their job, their kids, their grandkids, their car, their hobbies—pretty much anything they can think of. After an hour or so of this, all you can do is walk away thinking, *Man, they really didn't care about me at all*.

Few people have learned the true art of conversation in our culture. And it's so simple! Genuine, others-focused conversation all comes down to the ability to ask questions and listen to the answers. That's it. People who can do that, who actually show an interest in *getting to know you*, are generous people. They are highly attractive people. They are wise people, because they learn things that the rest of us who can't shut up never learn.

I think that's why *One Question* is such a jewel. My good friend Ken Coleman is a master conversationalist. He's learned not only how to ask questions and listen to the answers, but also how to ask *the right* questions and get the answers we all want to know. When you engage with other people at that level over several years, you end up with a long list of high-profile men and women who *want* to talk to you.

So, when Ken asked me to be part of this Who's Who of great contemporary thinkers, authors, and teachers, I was honored. As you scan through the table of contents, you'll see why it was such an honor. This book shows glimpses into Ken's conversations with people like Tony Dungee, Marcus Buckingham, Seth Godin, T.D. Jakes, Pat Summit, John C. Maxwell, Patrick Lencioni, Ken Blanchard, Malcolm Gladwell, and John McCain. When I see my name on that list, well, I sort of feel like a wiener in a steakhouse!

In today's publishing world, it wouldn't be unusual for an author to turn any one of these questions and answers into its own book with one good point surrounded by two hundred pages of fluff. That's not what you're getting here. In *One Question*, Ken hammers you with more than thirty powerful insights from some of the world's best leaders. Each chapter delivers the message quickly and succinctly, getting straight to the heart of the matter, and then moves on to the next powerful lesson.

When you get the chance to ask these great leaders one question, you get insights on how to live better, how to lead better, and generally how to *be* better. That's my prayer for you as you experience this fantastic book.

Always the beautiful answer who asks a more beautiful question.

—E. E. Cummings

Introduction

WHY ASK QUESTIONS?

Sweat beaded on my brow as I flipped through a stack of index cards, each scribbled with a single question. I was preparing to interview Duke University's head coach, Mike Krzyzewski. "Coach K," as fans affectionately call him, is a legend. He'd led the Blue Devils to four national championships and was elected to the Basketball Hall of Fame. There I was, a twenty-nine-year-old kid sitting on the home team's bench in Cameron Indoor Stadium, Duke University's storied basketball arena. For a Blue Devils fan like me, I was in Shangri-La.

I'd first encountered Duke basketball in 1986 while watching the team play the University of Louisville in the national championship. Sitting next to my dad, I was mesmerized by Duke's guards, Johnny Dawkins and Tommy Amaker. I could feel Coach K's intensity through the television as he worked the sideline. Duke lost 72 to 69 that night, but it won me over as a fan for life.

Two decades later, I sat on Coach K Court in a fit of nervousness—not just because I was about to interview my hero and one of the most successful coaches in the history of sport but also because it was my very first interview. Ever.

Originally, the seasoned Fox Sports commentator Bob Rathbun had been scheduled to do the interview, but he'd had to cancel at the last minute. I was the copy editor tasked with doing Bob's prep work for the segment, and that made me the only other person who knew enough to conduct the interview. The producer called my number.

The interview was scheduled for 10 A.M., and at 9:59 a door swung open. The arena's lights had been turned off for the interview, so I could barely make out the silhouette of a figure and hear the clip-clop of approaching shoes. Standing up, I reached out, shook Coach K's hand, and thanked him for giving us some of his time. He sat down, clipped on his mic, and it was go time.

I can't remember asking the first question. It was an icebreaker, and I must have been in an anxiety-induced trance. But I remember that, a few questions in, I finally settled down and the blood began to flow freely again. I transitioned naturally from question to question, surprising myself with a quick follow-up question every now and again when I wanted to know more.

I'd read his book, *Leading with the Heart*, prior to the interview, and many of the questions addressed the themes covered within. One idea from the book that intrigued me was when Coach K commented that he treats all his players "fair but not equal." He hadn't said much about it in the book, and I assumed he wanted it that way. I felt there was more to learn from that statement, so I asked him to paint a picture of what this meant.

He said he creates certain rules for the team and administers them fairly. But he doesn't treat everyone the same way. He began looking into the darkness of the arena, searching for the right example.

If a freshman was late for a bus departure, he said, he'd probably leave without him. But if a senior who had built up trust and rapport with the team was late, he'd probably wait on him. Then he brought up two of Duke's greatest point guards, Tommy Amaker and Bobby Hurley. Coach K said he would often draw up plays during a timeout for Tommy, and Tommy would run the play exactly as he'd been instructed. But Bobby was different. Bobby often changed the coach's play on the court. And Coach K gave Hurley that freedom because, he said, Bobby was built differently from Tommy. He was more instinctive, and even though he'd end up running a different play, it was always the right play.

"I treated both of them fairly," Coach K said, "but I didn't treat them equally."

Like a camera flash in a dark room, I suddenly realized the power of a single question. What had been a fairly mundane passage in this man's book had now taken on new life. When it came to Coach K, I was a walking Wikipedia page, but I now understood the power of his instincts, the scale of his leadership, and one of the keys to his legendary success.

Albert Einstein once said, "To raise new questions, new possibilities, to regard old problems from a new angle, requires creative imagination and marks real advance in science." What is true of science, I'm convinced, is true in all of life. Great questions are often the keys that unlock possibilities for human advancement. That truth has been proven again and again throughout human history, as great interviewers from Bob Costas to Barbara Walters have captivated audiences and ignited imaginations.

QUESTIONS REVEAL IMPORTANT THINGS

In a world where the messages of public figures and politicians are carefully crafted by publicists and media consultants, we often receive only partial pictures and manipulated facts. The right questions uncover truths we might not otherwise know. They pull back the curtain on the wizard and give us a more accurate view of reality.

Who can forget Katie Couric's interviews with vice presidential candidate Sarah Palin during the 2008 election? Until those interviews aired, Palin was trending positively among the American public. Though new to the national stage, many Americans found her to be likable. Then she sat down with Couric on the *CBS Evening News:*

COURIC: And when it comes to establishing your worldview, I was curious, what newspapers and magazines did you regularly read before you were tapped for this—to stay informed and to understand the world?

PALIN: I've read most of them again with a great appreciation for the press, for the media—

COURIC: But which ones specifically? I'm curious.

PALIN: Um, all of them, any of them that have been in front of me over all these years.

COURIC: Can you name any of them?

PALIN: I have a vast variety of sources where we get our news. Alaska isn't a foreign country, where, it's kind of suggested and it seems like, "Wow, how could you keep in touch with what the rest of Washington, D.C., may be thinking and doing when you live up there in Alaska?" Believe me, Alaska is like a microcosm of America.[1]

The mainstream media attacked the interview with ferocity. They criticized Palin's inability to offer an example of John McCain pushing for greater regulation, and they attacked her failure to name any Supreme Court decisions with which she disagreed. Many conservatives responded with criticisms of Couric and what was labeled "Gotcha journalism," but the media continued to chip away at Palin.

Regardless, that question in particular proved damaging, revealing what some perceived to be a lack of preparedness. Palin's answer spawned all the wrong sorts of headlines and marred her public image. Many political experts now cite that series of interviews as the turning point of the election.

QUESTIONS GET TO THE HEART OF A MATTER

Other people often tell us only what they want us to know or perhaps what they think we want to know, but not what we really need to know. Great leaders, in their memoirs, often share the stories they want to offer rather than the ones you'd like to hear. When you hear speeches by political candidates, they might disclose their answers to the problems they want to address but not the ones you care about. A great question is a surgeon's scalpel that cuts deep below the surface to tap into the issues behind the issues.

By 1974, former President Richard Nixon had spent more than two years away from public life. The public had been betrayed by the Watergate scandal, and most people felt that the way Nixon had addressed the subject had failed to deliver what Americans wanted to hear: either an admission of guilt or a public apology. But in 1977, Sir David Frost requested a series of interviews and Nixon accepted.

Both the public and the former president assumed that the interviews were nothing more than checkbook journalism. Nixon's slick responses rebuffed every attempt to get to the heart of the matter, but Frost continued to push with a sampling of great questions. Finally, Nixon cracked: "I let down my friends. I let down the country. I let down our system of government, and the dreams of all those young people that ought to get into government but now think it too corrupt. . . . I let the American people down, and I have to carry that burden with me the rest of my life."[2]

David Frost got the answer he'd been looking for, and the American people got exactly what they needed. Today, this interview is largely considered to be one of the greatest of the twentieth century.

QUESTIONS TRANSFORM

Occasionally, someone asks the right person the right question at the right time in the right way and magic happens: the person being interviewed moves beyond the mere facts to something deeper, something that flips a switch inside. The question produces an answer that inspires the interviewee, encourages him or makes him want to be a better person. It is in such moments that we discover a powerful maxim: good questions inform, but great questions transform.

Good questions inform, but great questions transform.

Perhaps the greatest model we have for questions that transform is not a modern journalist but an ancient rabbi. Jesus Christ was obsessed with asking questions, and, like many ancient rabbis, he would often answer questions with questions. But what set Jesus apart from other Jewish teachers is that he was able to do more than instruct; he was able to induce change. His questions didn't just reveal hidden truths or get to the heart of a matter; they also transformed all those who witnessed these encounters.

When religious leaders asked Jesus if they should pay taxes to the Roman government, he didn't respond with a simple yes or no. He held up a coin and asked, "Whose image is this?" (Matt. 22:17–20). When he reportedly broke religious laws and healed a man on the Jewish holy day, he was asked, "Is it lawful to heal on the Sabbath?" He responded with a single question: "If any of you has a sheep and it falls into a pit on the Sabbath, will you not take hold of it and lift it out?" (Matt. 12:9–12).

At first blush, contemporary observers may think that Jesus wasn't taking their questions seriously. But the opposite is true. He was validating the questions themselves, illustrating how probing rather than proving, and asking rather than arguing, often cuts a better path forward. With each query, he brought his audience's assumptions to the surface and forced them to wrestle with them. He challenged those around him to consider their thinking, presuppositions, and behaviors. The effect was so profound that people of faith have continued to wrestle with his questions for the last millennia, and many have walked away different from where they came.

Revealing, transformative answers to life's most important questions surge with power. Their wisdom can shape us, improve us, and carry us through every stage of life. When we are beginning our journey to success, they will help us discover who we are and unearth the calling that only we can fulfill. When the storms of life rage, they will sustain us like a levee. And once we find success—in our professional lives, home lives, and spiritual voyages—those answers will ensure that we hang on tight and finish well.

Back in Cameron Indoor Stadium, I sat knee to knee with Coach K as the camera crew took a break to change tapes. I began to realize that his profound answer to my singular question about being fair but not equal had done all three things every great question can do: It revealed what a great and thoughtful leader he was, even off the basketball court. It moved beyond the shallowness of his impressive win-loss record to get to the heart of why he's been so successful. And, perhaps most important, it changed me. I couldn't shake his words from my consciousness. In the years since, I've even incorporated his wisdom into the way I parent my children.

We sat in silence for a moment until he finally spoke. "I'm really enjoying this interview. This is one of the most enjoyable interviews I've ever done," he said. "You know, you really remind me of one of my best friends, Charlie Rose."

He went on to say that, like Charlie, I had an "uncanny ability to shoot the bull." But, he said, he meant that in a good way: we were both able to ask insightful questions in the natural flow of conversation.

I was slack-jawed at Coach K's comment—not just that he would make such a generous comparison but because he was validating a part of me I was just beginning to awaken to. Only minutes into the interview, I began realizing how much the experience was energizing me. "Maybe this is what I should be doing with my life," I thought.

After the interview concluded, he shook my hand and disappeared much as he'd entered. Standing in the arena that so many champions had called home, and having just spent time with one of my heroes, I was elated. Just before the crew had finished packing up our equipment, his assistant entered to tell us how much the coach had enjoyed his time with us. We responded that the pleasure was all ours.

Then she revealed a basketball and bounced it into my hands. "Before you go," she said, "why don't you take a shot?"

I was like a kid on Christmas morning! All smiles, I dribbled to the three-point line, eyed the rim, and released my shot into the air. As my feet touched back down, I knew the ball was on line and then heard the glorious *swish* as I watched the ball fall through the rim. I didn't even attempt to hold in my shout of joy. With my arms lifted high in triumph as I acknowledged the crew's applause and turned to walk off the court, I knew I'd found my life's calling.

Since that day, I've had the privilege of conducting hundreds of interviews with business leaders, celebrities, religious figures, bestselling authors, and music icons. I've been constantly astounded at how the right question—just one solitary question—can yield an unforgettable answer cram-packed with insight, wisdom, and encouragement for every stage of life. Many of those questions can be found in the pages that follow. A few are best kept in my heart for now. My hope is that they'll inspire you as much as they've inspired me, and perhaps they'll encourage you to answer your own nagging questions. After all, the secret of a killer interview is not just in the asking; it's also in the answer.

SUCCEEDING

one: Niche

John Maxwell
New York Times Bestselling Author

Agatha Christie's unique ability to weave intrigue and suspense into a web of excitement explains why she is the bestselling novelist of all time. Though she has been dead more than three decades, she has sold more than four billion copies of her books to date. I first experienced Christie's work when my high school drama teacher, Joy Bryant, chose *The Mousetrap* as our spring play my junior year. The murder mystery holds the honor of being the longest-running show of the modern era.

When the announcement was made, I determined that I would audition for the lead role, Detective Sergeant Trotter. I wanted to be a star, and it seemed the best way for my seventeen-year-old self to realize it. When I arrived for the audition, however, Ms. Bryant threw me a curveball. She asked me also to read for the part of Christopher Wren. Confused and feeling slighted, I reluctantly agreed.

My anticipation mounted for the next two days as I waited for the announcement to be made. When the list was posted, I rushed down the hall and ran my finger down the paper. There it was for all to see: "Ken Coleman—Christopher Wren." My disappointment was difficult to hide.

After class, I waited around to confront Ms. Bryant on her poor casting ability.

"I know you wanted the lead role," she said. "But you are perfect for Wren. No one in this school can play him like you can, and you will notice, if you read the script, that he steals the show. Just trust me."

Christopher Wren is the mad character that Christie added for comedic relief. I recognized the prominence given to him in the script, but I didn't care what he was. I was only concerned with what he wasn't: the lead. After sulking and mulling for several days, I decided to give the role my best.

No one perhaps has spoken more about playing the role you were meant to play than John Maxwell. He is a *New York Times* bestselling author of cornerstone leadership books, including *Developing the Leader Within You, Make Today Count,* and *The 21 Irrefutable Laws of Leadership*. His mission in life is to equip people to identify their strengths and maximize their effectiveness as influencers. When I had the opportunity to ask him one question, I decided to frame it around the subject of niche.

KC: My father said to me over and over as a kid, "Find your niche and fill it." We all have unique talents and strengths, yet so many never find their niche. How do we find it?

JM: My father helped us a lot too. He was very committed to his gifts and used them well. As we grew up, he basically told us the same thing: "Find the one thing you do well, and do it. You are not able to do twenty things well, so find the one thing that you do well." So when people come to me about their niche, I always ask them two questions. One is "What are you passionate about?" And number two is "What are you good at?"

I have known a lot of people who are very passionate about things they are not good at. So the good news is they really loved what they were doing, and the bad news was that they were not any good at it.

I have known people who were very good at something, but they were not passionate about it. So the good news was that they were really good at it, and the bad news is they could not stick with it. They could not even stay in their sweet spot, because they did not have the passion for it. So it is not either/or, it is both/and.

Once you can answer, "What am I passionate about?" and "What am I good at?" you can marry those two things. Then you have the energy to take you over the long haul to be the person that you really want to be. When people are doing one thing *but* would like to go do something else, my whole advice is then "Quit but-ing and start going."

My advice to a lot of people when they come to me and say, "What do you think I ought to do? I am getting worn out with this" is "Quit." And then they will say, "What do you mean, quit?" I say again, "Quit. You have to stop doing what you are doing today if it is not effective, or you do not enjoy it, to be able to start doing what you want to do, tomorrow." That takes a little bit of security, but I do think that is the key.

You really have to love what you do. I cannot imagine anybody, every day, going to work just because he has to go to work, and just kind of filling in the day with something he does not love. People who do not love what they are doing are Cape Canaveral people: ten, nine, eight, seven, six. . . . They are counting down before they can quit work. They are counting down before they can stop that relationship. I say, "You ought to be counting up, not counting down. You ought to be going up." So put your passions and your gifts together, and then you have found something.

Maxwell gives us a simple but profound equation: passions + gifts = niche. Some people label this "calling," but the moniker doesn't matter as much as the principle. Too many people live lives of desperation and dissatisfaction, but we all possess the road map for the way out of that gloomy town.

When you operate outside your niche, you'll end up being one of two types of people. First, you may become a person who is good at his job but not passionate about it. This is, for example, the corporate marketing executive who is talented at crafting a message and knows the company's needs well. He makes a great living and has a beautiful office atop a tall tower. But he is wasting away.

My friend was a lead Web designer for a large corporation, making hundreds of thousands of dollars a year. He was great at his job, but he needed a client he could believe in. One day, he simply quit his job and moved to Maui, where he now designs small websites for nonprofits. You may be working a nine-to-five in accounting or customer care or insurance sales, but your heart desires to go work with special-needs kids. Like Maxwell, I'd tell you, "Go work with special-needs children."

The second type of person is passionate about his job but not good at it. You see him on reality talent shows every day. He loves to sing, but he doesn't have the talent to carry it. You wince when confusion washes over his face after he's told he is "pitchy." Lack of talent is only a symptom; the real problem is a failure to identify his niche. You won't be your happiest or most effective until you can find a place where you are *both* passionate and talented.

I'd add another subcategory to Maxwell's list. This is a person who has identified both his passions and his gifts but lacks the backbone to make a change. Once we locate our niche, we need the courage and discipline to pursue it. If you find and fill your niche, you'll never "work" another day in your life.

If you find and fill your niche, you'll never "work" another day in your life.

Flashback to opening night of *The Mousetrap*. The cast is pacing backstage, driven by our collective nervousness. We have two back-to-back shows, and both are sold out. When I take the stage, I feel a surge of another person in my veins. I deliver my lines, not as Ken but as Christopher Wren. As Ms. Bryant predicted, I steal the show and earn a roar of applause at the end of each performance.

Driving home that night, I realized that Ms. Bryant had been teaching me about more than just acting. She was instructing me on niche: you need to know who you are, and you need to play your role to the best of your ability. My drama teacher knew me better than I knew myself, and she handed me a valuable life lesson that I will teach my three kids.

The spotlight now turns to you. Have you found your niche, and are you filling it? If not, what are you going to do about it?

Play the role that only you can, the one you were born for. If you marry your passions and gifts, when the curtain closes and you wait for a response, you'll find you've done more for the audience than you ever imagined you could.

two: Strengths

Marcus Buckingham
New York Times Bestselling Author

Shortly after my wife, Stacy, and I welcomed our second child, we realized that every child is different. Each one is custom designed, filled with unique gifts, talents, strengths, and passions. We have three children: Ty (seven), Chase (five), and Josie (four). All three are exceptional human beings in their own way.

I've always believed that parenting is more than guiding kids into adulthood; it's getting them ready to launch. One day my children will shed tears from their first broken heart and know the frustration of a significant failure. My role as their father is to partner with my wife in preparing them for those moments so when the troubles of life strike, they'll know who they are and why they were placed on this earth.

Marcus Buckingham is a leading voice on the subjects of strengths and succeeding. He came barreling into the public eye when his 1999 book, *First, Break All the Rules*, conquered the bestseller lists. He then went on to help create StrengthsFinder, a personal assessment tool that gave millions of individuals a new vocabulary to positively describe their ingrained talents. In addition to refining and reinforcing his message in subsequent books, he founded the Marcus Buckingham Company in 2007 to assist managers and organizations in accessing the untapped potential of their people's strengths.

As a personal-growth junkie, I have come to admire Buckingham's counterintuitive message of focusing on our strengths instead of trying to improve upon our weaknesses. As a father of three, I wanted to know if his principles could be applied to rearing children. One of the earliest indicators of a child's strengths and passions is his academic performance in grade school. I wanted to know if Buckingham thought that applying his philosophy early on in a child's life might prepare that child for a smoother and more successful launch into adulthood.

KC: When a child brings home a C, a D, or an F, what should the parental response be in light of what you believe about focusing on one's strengths?

MB: Well, I think there are three things that you have to do when a child brings home an A, B, C, D, and F. The first is that you have to spend more time on the As. You don't have to praise the child, although that is fine. This isn't about building self-esteem with your kid, it's about trying to understand how the kid learns. Ask, "Why are you interested in that subject? What is it about that subject that gets you going? Do you find it easy? Which bits do you find easy? Is it the teacher? What is it about the teacher?" Don't grill your child, but if your kid is bringing back As, any parent needs to become really familiar with why: "Did you just work harder? Why did you work harder? Was it the textbook?"

It's a wonderful source of conversation with your kid. That's the power of positive focus—"What happened there? Let's look at that. That worked—why?"

The second thing, you can't ignore the F. If your kid gets an F in math, it's for one of two reasons. One is that he is bad in math, and the other is that he is good in math but badly taught. Either way, the answer to what you do with that is through the As. By studying the As, you might find out that your kid learns in a particular way. The kid learns by doing, not by sitting there and watching a blackboard with a bunch of equations on it. The kid learns by practicing, by trial and error. You can apply that knowledge to the F and see whether or not you get any improvement, because maybe, just maybe, taking the lessons about how the kid learns for an A can be directly applied to how the kid learns for an F.

Or maybe you find out that the kid just has absolutely no—no matter how he is taught—affinity for math at all. In which case, now at least both of you know that. Together, you and your kid can figure out a way to manage around the fact that the F is there, so that it doesn't undermine every conversation you ever have. It might be simply saying, "We are going to spend just a little time together to make sure that that F is a C, so it doesn't hold you back. But my expectations of you, son, aren't going to be that you turn that F into A, because now we've worked on that a little bit, and now we know it's not that you're good at math and badly taught, it's just that numbers and you are strangers. So let's just figure out how you can make sure that it doesn't trip you up." That is useful: your kid now is aware that you are aware of what he was always aware of.

The last thing is that you tell your kid to experiment—keep trying stuff out to improve the grade. It could be that that F is an F because you just started working on it together. Maybe keep trying a little bit, because sometimes kids quit too early. They try, they get bored, and they move on.

But that's okay too. Some parents are focus junkies. We say, "Well, he tried tennis and he gave up after four lessons. Tried piano—gave up after four classes. This is terrible!" No, it's called being a child. Make sure you end up with your kid zeroing in on his strengths, so he's had a chance to touch and feel and try things out. That kind of inquisitiveness defines us as human beings.

> "Make sure you end up with your kid zeroing in on his strengths, so he's had a chance to touch and feel and try things out. That kind of inquisitiveness defines us as human beings."

Buckingham's words seemed to make sense at the time, but they've really proved true since Ty entered elementary school. Rather than concentrating on his weakest subjects and creating frustrated mediocrity, I'm focusing the same energy on his strengths, ensuring that he'll excel in the areas in which he's truly gifted. Our progress-oriented society has ingrained into our heads that we need to work harder to improve our weaknesses, and this way of thinking has affected both our parenting style and the development of our children. Buckingham's advice is both practical for observing and communicating with our children and powerful for preparing our children to find their passions and fulfill their purposes in life.

In teaching us about our children, Buckingham also teaches us about ourselves. In an attempt to discover their life's calling, many people wait around to see a flash of light or awake to the voice of God at two or three in the morning. Buckingham reminds us that our calling isn't something we have to search for relentlessly; it's sewn into who we are. As we recognize our strengths, we'll uncover our passions. Where our strengths intersect our passions, therein lies our calling. We do well to discern ours in adulthood and even better to help our children discover theirs before we launch them into an untamed world.

three: Connecting

Peter Guber
CEO of Mandalay Entertainment and *New York Times*
Bestselling Author

Nervousness hung in the greenroom like wallpaper. Acquaintances traded forced comments to fill space, but all eyes conspicuously watched the door. Mikhail Gorbachev had spoken at the leadership summit earlier that day, as had hip-hop mogul Russell Simmons and international bestselling authors Peter Drucker and Ken Blanchard. But we were all waiting for the event's most anticipated speaker to arrive. Everyone wanted to know what Donald Trump was really like.

Having watched Trump on *The Apprentice* and in several media interviews, I wondered how he'd gotten anywhere in life. He seemed arrogant and disagreeable, bullheaded and impossible to work with. The Manhattan billionaire's greatest joy in life, I surmised, was firing employees. He'd become famous for it.

Stacy and I were in midconversation when Trump strolled into the room accompanied by his bodyguard, a man who looked like a former roughneck cop from the Bronx. Like the others, we fell silent and turned toward him. Trump paused. He scanned the room, looking each person in the eyes. And then he smiled.

"Hello, everyone," he said with genuine kindness.

The room exhaled a sigh of relief as Trump began working his way through the crowd. Many speakers that day preferred to sit on a corner couch, where they would not be bothered. But not Trump. He sauntered around the room, greeting each person and posing for pictures with the staff. When he met Stacy and me, the cameraman needed to change film. Trump waited patiently, asking my wife questions about our life. He was larger than life, inflated by confidence but held to earth by a surprising authenticity. Moments later, Trump headed to the stage, where he would speak to participants in the arena and others simulcasting in ninety-five cities and two dozen countries. The greenroom crowd was left breathless and energized.

Stacy and I left that day with a picture of ourselves with "The Donald." We sent it out as our Christmas card that year with the text "I bet our Christmas card Trumps yours." But our most important keepsake from this encounter was not a photograph; it was a lesson on success from one of America's premier businessmen. Donald Trump was nothing like his television persona, the barbarian dream maker and deal breaker. He knew how to touch people, to make them feel important.

On the drive home, my wife asked me what about Donald Trump had impressed me the most.

"He is not a great speaker," I replied, "but he is a master at connecting with people."

Peter Guber also knows a bit about connecting with people. As the CEO of the Mandalay Entertainment Group, he's produced such touching films as *Rain Man*, *The Color Purple*, and *Flashdance*. His films have earned more than $3 billion worldwide and garnered fifty Academy Award nominations. His book, *Tell to Win: Connect, Persuade, and Triumph with the Hidden Power of Story*, became a number one *New York Times* bestseller. I decided to ask Guber the secrets of connecting with others.

KC: We communicate with each other every day through speaking, writing, and body language. But those who go beyond communication to form meaningful connections seem to go much farther, much faster. How can we master the art of connecting?

PG: Connecting is deeper and more lasting than just communicating. When you are communicating, one person has to speak and the other has to hear. But when you are connecting, the intention of the speech and the speaker, and the intention of the listener and how empathetically he actually listens, actually matter. Connecting is not aimed at intellectual capital; it is aimed at emotional resources. To connect, one must aim for the heart, not the wallet. And this will build relationships that endure, not merely fleeting transactions.

Communication seeks to call into action, to get the listener to do something: vote for me, buy my product, come work in my company, be my friend, go on a trip with me. You have a goal. The reason we invented language was to create social cohesion and the environment where people could depose ideas and socially organize so they could get things done. But connecting is deeper, more lasting, and actually more intuitive than communicating.

If you intend to connect, then you are already transmitting before you speak the first word. You are already sending a signal, and what you are sending is your intention, your etheric or authentic self. And to be authentic, you must be congruent. Before you speak the first word, you must align your heart with your time and your wallet and your feet. And that means setting up your intention before you try to get the other party's attention.

You see this in any type of activity, in all of life. It's called the "get in" state. When you walk into a meeting, you have to create that "get in" state. You have to create that congruence, that intention, that authenticity before you speak the words. Intention must precede attention. It gives emotional propulsion to the data, facts, and analysis.

Second, you must be audience-centric. I say *audience* rather than *customer*, *client*, or *patron* because customers, clients, and patrons protect their wallets. Audiences open their hearts. If you are trying to create that movement, you have to keep hearts open. It is, in fact, a sort of a Trojan horse to give you information. Focus on what is in it for them, not what is in it for you. It's not what you want, but what do they want? Not what the benefit is to you, what is the benefit to them? And if you are trying to trick them, you are in trouble because they will perceive dishonesty. They will perceive a lack of integrity. They will perceive a lack of congruence, so all the words will fall on infertile soil.

The next thing you have also to think about is the call to action. Before you walk into the room, before you send the email or the text, before you talk on the phone, before you get up in front of the group, you have to know what the call to action is. What do you want them to do with the communication: love you, marry you, have sex with you, give you money, join your company, start their company, get a raise, get a promotion, become an advocate of something? What is your goal? If you cannot state it quickly on a rainy night and at sixty miles per hour, then do not go into the room or send the text or send the email. Go have some popcorn and sit and relax in your Barca-lounger.

Also, you should know that the more generous the goal, the better it is. The clearer the goal, the better it is. Hiding the goal is terrible. Not having skin in the game or not shining light on the goal due to the risk is terrible. That is what creates integrity and authenticity—exposing both the goal and risk—and those things will get the audience to take a risk. If you do not, they will not do it.

And one of the last elements is to remember that all communication is a dialogue, not a monologue. When it is a monologue, it is only pitching, not pitching and catching. It leaves no space for the other person to become a participant. The person in the audience becomes a passenger. And in our interactive world, being a passenger is being a loser. You want the person listening to participate, to take a risk, to invest, to be an evangelizer, or to become an advocate for your offering. The audience has to own it. The more they own it, the more the physiology changes. The more dialogue, not monologue, the more the audience will own their commitment to your call, the more they will remember it. The more resonant and memorable, the greater the call to action will be.

> "Intention must precede attention. It gives emotional propulsion to the data, facts, and analysis."

Where there is laughing, asking questions, good talking, empathetic listening, and looking at the signals of the other person—not just their words but also their eyes—the better and deeper the connection will be. The next time the person meets you, he will bring that experience to the meeting. He may not like your product, he may not want to buy your business this time, but he will come into the room next time and be open. He will get in before you get there.

Finally, remember that you cannot guarantee the result. Surrender the certainty of result.

Guber reminds us that connecting is as much a function of the state of our hearts as of our heads. In order to open an audience's hearts, ours must be in the right place. As he put it, "If you are trying to trick them, you are in trouble because they will perceive dishonesty. They will perceive a lack of integrity."

You cannot connect with others unless you can establish trust. If you value others only for what they can give you, they'll sense it. It is the difference in the feeling you get from being around a pastor making a hospital visit and being around a used-car salesman who smells the scent of a pending sale. The former disarms you; the latter forces you into a defensive posture. One of the best things you can do to connect with others is to check the state of your own heart, to expose and eliminate your ulterior motives.

Once we establish trust, we must draw our audience into the conversation. Make them participants, Guber says, not passengers. Leaders often assume that success depends on what we say and how well we say it. But success often depends on what we do when we are not talking. Learn to listen with your eyes by reading the body language of those with whom you are communicating. Ask open-ended questions. If you can turn the audience into participants rather than passengers, you'll increase the chance that they'll receive your message rather than reject it.

We must learn the art of conversation, to dance with those we encounter, to care more about the person we're speaking to than the goal we want to accomplish. If you can master the art of connecting in life, you'll go farther and faster.

four: Authenticity

Randall Wallace
Oscar-Nominated Screenwriter

When Stacy and I moved to Nashville, we had no idea what America's Music City had in store for us. We bought our first house, grew closer as a couple, and met lifelong friends there. At the time, I was working as an agent for one of the top speakers' bureaus in the nation. Between cutting deals for my clientele, which included bestselling authors, politicians, musicians, and athletes, I was scouting the countryside for undiscovered talent.

One day, a client called me to tell me about a comedian friend of his in whom I might be interested. Not thinking much of the request, I asked him to send me a highlight reel of his friend's act. A few days later the DVD arrived, and I decided to take a look at it over lunch. A few bites into my ham sandwich, I chuckled. A couple more, and I started to choke. I was soon laughing uncontrollably. Jumping up, I stopped the DVD and asked my boss and a few other agents to join me. Their experience was identical to mine, and after forty-five minutes, our sides were hurting and we had broken into sweat from laughter.

Rather than wait, I phoned the comedian that day. A few minutes into our conversation, he shared his frustrations with me. He'd been playing the club scene in Los Angeles, and though he wasn't starving, he wasn't thriving either. His vision was to do family-friendly comedy, without curse words or gratuitous sexual jokes, an uncommon package to sell to L.A. nightclubs. He was worried that he might not be able to take his act to the next level without compromising who he was.

"Don't change who you are to 'make it,'" I told him. "You're funny, and there is a place for you in this business. You need to be who you are because no one else is like you."

I suggested he move to Nashville because I thought he'd have a stronger base among the South's more conservative and religious audiences. Red-state clubs could push him into the spotlight. He took my advice, moved to Nashville having never met me, and our bureau signed him. Within months, his family-friendly George-Carlin-meet-Robin-Williams act took off.

The comedian was Brad Stine, and his act has since been featured on outlets such as HBO, Showtime, Comedy Central, and MTV. After moving to Nashville, he released a comedy album and thanked three people on the jacket: his mom, his wife, and me. Yet I didn't feel as if I had earned the kudos. I hadn't discovered Stine; I had just encouraged him to discover who he was meant to be. He deserves credit for finding the courage not to compromise who he is.

Another uncompromising figure in my mind is the Hollywood screenwriter Randall Wallace. In a town that seems to change all those who enter it, Wallace has remained true to himself. He's set out to create films imbued with virtue and inspiration. From *Pearl Harbor* to *We Were Soldiers* to *Braveheart*, he's done just that. Sitting down with the Oscar-nominated artist, I wanted to ask him about the importance of staying true to ourselves even as we pursue our dreams.

KC: Many screenwriters have moved to Hollywood and lost themselves, but you seem to have maintained authenticity throughout the years. If you could share one lesson with budding professionals and storytellers on how to succeed without compromising who they are, what would it be?

RW: Tell a story that moves you, and if it does not move you, change the story until it does. The turning point in my career as a writer in Hollywood came when I realized that if I tried to tell stories based just on what I thought Hollywood wanted to buy, then I had lost my soul already. I'd been working as a writer-producer for a thriving company when the Writers Guild went on strike.

The strike went on forever, and when it was over the company was barely there anymore. I was out of work, my savings were gone, and I was sitting at my desk one day trying to write, my stomach in a knot, my hands trembling, and I realized I was breaking down.

I feared I had failed my father, my mother, and my grandmother. And my greatest fear was that I would fail my sons. I was afraid they would see me come apart, and it would be something they could never forget. I got down on my knees; I had nowhere else to go. And I prayed a simple prayer: "Lord, all I care about right now are those two boys. And maybe they don't need to grow up in a house with a tennis court and a swimming pool. Maybe they need a little house with one bathroom, or no bathrooms at all. Maybe they need to see what a man does when he gets knocked down, the way my father showed me. But I pray, if I go down, let me go down not on my knees praying to a false idol trying to sell what I think Hollywood wants, but instead with my flag flying." And I got up, and I began to write the words that led me to *Braveheart*.

I want to tell the stories that give me goose bumps, that make my heart vibrate with a sense of life, as if God has chimed the tuning fork in me and no matter what the outcome, I will be fine with it. My advice to young storytellers: be authentic and tell the story that resonates in your soul.

As with Wallace, the desire to succeed and the pressures of life often force us to flirt with compromising who we are. As ambitious twenty-two-year-olds, we often possess well-defined visions for how we want to pursue our callings. Yet somewhere along the way, as we amass spouses and children and debt, our dreams become far more pragmatic. We can lose ourselves as life happens. Wallace's words call us to recommit ourselves to authenticity.

In all endeavors, the audience, clients, customers, and patrons must be considered. But pleasing them is not the ultimate goal. You can't consider your audience first and *then* find your message. Instead, you must find the message inside of you and then craft that message to speak to a particular audience. The movement of your life has to flow from the inside out, rather than the outside in. Many people say, "This is what I want to be" and then attempt to reverse engineer themselves to become that. The Beatles didn't approach their craft by saying "We want to write hit songs." They found their unique melodies and produced sounds unlike anyone else's. Because they chose to be who they alone could be, they were able to rise higher than they'd ever imagined.

Though it might surprise you, a sure path to success is to be who you are. We live in a world of carbon copies, but there is only one you. Unleashing your authentic self is the best way to pierce the noise and rise above the pack. Even if your message sounds like someone else's, the way you speak that message will be unique. We fail when we try to become someone else, when we allow our insecurities or external influences to convince us to become people we aren't. You must live your life with the belief that there's a space only you can fill.

It took years for someone to pick up *Braveheart*; then Mel Gibson got his hands on it. It may take time for you to gain traction in your own calling. Be who you were meant to be. Even if you stumble, you'll go down with your flag flying. And that's a success in itself.

five: Opportunity

Seth Godin
New York Times Bestselling Author

The jarring line flooded my Twitter feed on October 5, 2011: "RIP Steve Jobs." The innovator's battle with cancer had been widely publicized, but few had embraced the reality that he'd be gone so soon. Jobs had become a fixture in American life, wowing the world with regularity by showcasing industry-changing devices. We'd assumed that he, like other icons, would always be there. The news of his death was a splash of cold water in millions of faces.

I wasn't grieved that day. Pensive, maybe. I'd never personally connected with Jobs as I had with his devices. I wrestled with the feeling one gets when any personality passes on. The thought that America's most famous innovator would never invent again left me awestruck, solemn, and reflective.

I began wandering the Web, searching for commentary on the impact of Jobs's death. Some observers were listing him in the ranks of Albert Einstein and Thomas Edison. Others seemed to believe that his influence had been exaggerated. The irony that I was reading both perspectives on a mobile phone that Jobs had created was not lost on me.

Clicking a hyperlink in one article, I was whisked away to a piece about Apple's twelfth employee, Mark Stephens. In 1977, Mark helped Jobs and Steve Wozniak move out of a garage and into an office. "The Steves" struggled to generate much profit from their new start-up, leading them to offer Stephens a unique proposition.

"Steve Jobs didn't have much cash, so he tried to pay people like me in stock," Stephens said. "But I held out for cash—I think six dollars an hour at the time. It was, uh, a big mistake."[1]

The staggering misstep gave me pause. Stephens was given a once-in-a-lifetime opportunity, though he didn't recognize it at the time, and he passed it up. Sure, Jobs was clearly a visionary with great ideas. But taking a stock option would be risky, and choosing a paycheck was a safe bet. Focused on the immediate, he missed out on an amazing future that had been laid in his lap. The palm-on-forehead moment plagues him to this day.

As I read the article, I commented to myself on Stephens's misfortune. Instead of recognizing the opportunity before him, he had taken a safe path. He had lost out on millions of dollars as a result. As I was castigating Stephens in my mind, however, I realized that he is no different from the rest of us. We all miss out on great opportunities in life. The only difference is that the person who offered Stephens his turned out to be one of America's greatest innovators. Like us, Stephens couldn't *seize* the opportunity because he couldn't *see* it.

No one speaks more affably about seizing opportunity than does Seth Godin, the author of thirteen bestselling books, including *Lynchpin*, *Tribes*, and *Purple Cow*. An entrepreneur and former VP of Yahoo!, Godin encourages his readers to recognize prospects and leverage them to spread their ideas. Having just learned of Jobs's death and Stephens's mistake, I decided to ask him about seizing opportunities.

KC: There can be no success without opportunity, but finding it and seizing it can sometimes be difficult. How can we best discern which opportunities to take and then maximize them?

SG: Why do some people see opportunity when others miss it? It's obvious that our lives are overflowing with opportunity: the opportunity to connect, to lead, to make a difference in someone's life. We have the opportunity to start, finish, and even invent.

And yet, most of the time, most of us are blind to what's possible. The reason is simple: we're afraid.

Fear is the flip side of opportunity. You can't have one without the other, because opportunity represents change, and change, for all organisms, means flirting with death. From an evolutionary standpoint, change is the enemy, because change brings risk.

Fear is our compass. It's overrated as an effective warning tool, but in our culture, right now, the best opportunities all carry the same warning. Until you've adopted a posture that change is good and fear is part of the deal, you'll remain paralyzed.

Once you've shifted, though, choices become a lot clearer. Instead of seeking out a path that has no risk, realize that you've already signed up for risk and now your job is to find the best path, not the fear-free path.

Godin notes that "most of us are blind to what's possible," and I know he's right. I can count several opportunities that, when I was a young person, sailed out of my life untouched and unnoticed. Had I accessed Godin's wisdom decades ago, many headaches and heartaches might have been averted.

Many people sleep through life, unaware of the opportunities that drift by their doorsteps. They aren't waiting, aren't watching, aren't ready for them. As Coach John Wooden once said, "When opportunity comes, it's too late to prepare." So we need to open our eyes and raise our antennas to the possibilities around us.

But in addition to *seeing* opportunities, we need to *seize* them when they come. Many times we recognize our potential, but we waste it. Perhaps we've grown comfortable in the life we've built. Or maybe we've chosen to wander through life rather than intentionally chart a course that moves us beyond where we sit. Often, Godin says, fear is our compass. We don't have enough confidence in our life's calling to overcome the

> **Many people sleep through life, unaware of the opportunities that drift by their doorsteps.**

anxiety that accompanies big decisions. Because we don't know the consequences a decision will bring, we may choose to remain in the present.

Though we cannot know the future, we can decide which future we'll pursue. Once we see clearly where we're going, we'll be looking for the waypoints of opportunity that will move us further down the road.

If you know who you are and what you are supposed to do in life, you will live fully awake, eyes wide open. Scout for opportunities as they materialize around you. But remember that merely recognizing that an opportunity exists is not enough. When it comes, we must make the dangerous decision to throw down our red capes, grab the opportunity by the horns, and drag it to the arena floor.

six: Vision

T. D. Jakes
Pastor and *New York Times* Bestselling Author

Moneyball fascinated moviegoers across the United States. I watched the film only after I'd heard that it had been nominated for six Oscars, including Best Motion Picture. The storyline shocked many, but it was old news to me. I'm a die-hard sports fan who grew up watching the Atlanta Braves as a child. The TBS network broadcast their games around the country, making them America's team. I idolized Braves greats of the era such as Dale Murphy and Brett Butler and was a passionate baseball card collector. I've also subscribed to *Sports Illustrated* for more than two decades, so I observed the tale of Billy Beane as it unfolded in real time.

A former Major League Baseball player, Beane became the general manager of the Oakland Athletics in 1997. After losing to the New York Yankees in the 2001 play-offs, he realized that the cash-poor A's would never compete with wealthier teams unless he could find a competitive advantage. That's when Beane met Peter Brand, a recent Yale graduate who evaluated players using statistical formulas. Beane and Brand decided to assemble a team of unsung players with a proven ability to get on base and score runs.

Beane's scouts protested the unorthodox move and spent the season working against his system, but Beane persisted in circumventing their efforts and proving he was right. The Athletics struggled early in the season but found their step and set an American League record by winning an unprecedented twenty consecutive games. Though Beane's team lost in the postseason, Major League Baseball recognized the wisdom in his new system. America's favorite pastime was revolutionized forever, and today, nearly every Major League Baseball team employs an Ivy League number cruncher.

The story was immortalized in *Moneyball*, Michael Lewis's 2003 book on baseball economics and the film starring Brad Pitt. When I first saw the movie, I was filled with nostalgia. With each turn in the plot, my mind flashed back to the *Sports Illustrated* feature stories debating the vitality of Beane's risky decisions. The credits finally scrolled and I snapped back into reality, recognizing that the film was far more than a good sports movie; it was a valuable lesson on visionary leadership.

By taking a new approach to baseball management, Billy Beane opposed the odds in a career where odds are everything. He risked losing his reputation, even his job, if the plan didn't work. But because he believed in the revolutionary system, he cast a bold vision for the future. Eventually, others lined up behind his leadership.

How does a leader effectively cast a vision, and what inspires others to follow it? This question haunted me after watching *Moneyball*, and I decided to seek out an inspirational "visioneer." Thomas Dexter "T. D." Jakes is something of a jack-of-all-trades. He is the pastor of the Potter's House, a thirty-thousand-member congregation in Dallas, Texas, but his influence stretches well outside of the church. He's produced films grossing in the tens of millions of dollars and is a *New York Times* bestselling author, and his television show, *The Potter's Touch*, airs nationwide on stations including BET. In 2005, he was named one of the twenty-five most influential evangelicals in America by *Time* magazine. The publication had featured him on its cover just four years earlier with the headline "Is This Man the Next Billy Graham?" Jakes knows how to cast a vision like few others, and everything he touches seems to flourish. I wanted to know what he thought about this critical leadership skill.

KC: If you were going to teach a class on casting vision, what would you tell your students are the mandatory ingredients of this vital leadership responsibility?

TJ: To be innovative in their thought process rather than to accept the status quo. I think that the earmark of a leader is somebody who goes where others have not gone, who blazes trails and conquers new horizons with his thinking. Many leaders throughout our country's history have done this. They're the ones who have built railroads where there was wilderness, who dreamed of building an aircraft and helping it sail across the sky, who dreamed of packaging electricity into a lightbulb or putting technology into a computer. These are the people who have really moved our civilization forward, the trailblazers and not imitators. And I think we have a great deficit today in that we have too many people who have lost their ability to innovate and trailblaze and instead have become voices echoing what others have already done.

Jakes points out that one of a visionary's greatest characteristics is courage. They see what others cannot see and go where others dare not tread. I think of George Washington envisioning a new nation or Walt Disney envisioning an entertainment wonderland while looking down on a swamp. Visionary leaders challenge others to join them in a journey to an uninhabited destination by way of an unknown path. Machete in hand, they clear a path into the virgin jungle.

> **Visionaries see beyond what *is* and picture what *could* be or *should* be.**

Though visionary leaders know that a problem exists, they may not know right away how to solve it. But they are driven by the belief that a solution must exist, that a solution always exists. So visionaries begin looking for alternate paths, for new and better courses. They see beyond what *is* and picture what *could* or *should* be.

The courage of these leaders almost always draws resistance. Many times when you outline a vision, you're asking people to believe in something only you can see. When everyone else relies on insight, visionaries rely on imagination. While others nestle comfortably into the status quo, visionaries upset the apple cart. They're adept at finding and solving problems when others either fail to recognize them or have long since accepted that they are unsolvable. Followers look at a problem and get bothered; visionaries look at a problem and get busy. The disparity makes others uncomfortable.

When great visionaries prove they are right, however, the masses come around. In Beane's case, his scouts bought in, and all of baseball took note. The Boston Red Sox brought in Beane and offered him a job, but after much thought, he turned them down. The Red Sox wanted to replicate Oakland's system, but Beane wasn't a replicator. He was a trailblazer. And that's just the point: visionaries always are.

seven: Dreams

Blake Mycoskie
Founder of TOMS Shoes and *New York Times* Bestselling Author

"Ken, you got a minute?" my friend Charlie asks. I see the glimmer in his eye that I recognize all too well. Charlie wants to talk to me about his dream for a new business venture. We've been discussing his vision for more than three years now, and I muster all the enthusiasm I have left, trying not to express how tired I am of hearing about it.

Sadly, Charlie's dream is quite good. He's bright and capable, and he knows how to deliver a rousing presentation. He's identified a distinct audience. He possesses the creative capacity to deliver. And there is a real need for his proposed product. But each time we discuss the next steps, they never get done. Will his dream ever materialize? I have my doubts. The potential is there, but something is missing.

You may know people like Charlie. They catch a vision while sipping a cup of coffee or soaking in the evening news. As the idea develops, they begin to leak it to their family and close friends. Soon they are meeting with others in related industries to dream out loud. Then things begin to sputter. A year later, the dream is on the back burner or perhaps a distant memory.

In grade school, being a "dreamer" was a negative. It was a label teachers used to tell parents that their children lacked focus. The title in adulthood, however, has a positive connotation. People want a leader who will dream big and cast ambitious visions for an organization. But Charlie makes me wonder if our teachers were on to something. Not that being a dreamer is totally negative, but rather that real work never gets done if we live in the creative clouds. We must learn to drag our ideas out of the stratosphere and down to the street level if we ever hope to realize them.

My growing frustration with Charlie inspired the one question I asked Blake Mycoskie, the founder of TOMS Shoes. He is a dreamer—he lives on a sailboat in Los Angeles—but he's the kind who gets things done. Before launching TOMS, he started five businesses, including an online driver education company and a successful national campus laundry service. Always the competitor, he competed in the CBS series *The Amazing Race* and came within minutes of earning the $1 million grand prize.

While visiting Argentina during *The Amazing Race*, Mycoskie birthed an ambitious dream. In January 2006, he decided to start a shoe company where, for every pair sold, he would donate a pair of shoes to a needy child. The one-for-one model resonated with many in the American marketplace, and today TOMS are sold in more than five hundred stores across the country, including Nordstrom, Whole Foods, and Neiman Marcus. TOMS has donated more than two million pairs of shoes to date. Mycoskie's book, *Start Something That Matters*, was a bestseller. I decided to ask him what he believed was the key to realizing one's dreams.

KC: What would you say to people who have a big idea but are full of anxiety because they do not know where to start or how to get going? How can they begin to make their dreams a reality?

BM: One of the things I think is really important is this idea of starting small. When I started TOMS, my goal was to help 250 kids. Just 250 kids. I did not quit my job, I did not go out and raise a bunch of money, and I did not spend a year working on a business plan. I saw that there was this need in Argentina, and I wanted to help these 250 kids in a sustainable way.

I was concerned that these kids needed shoes and that the need was completely dependent on donations. I did not want them to be wondering when and where they would get their next pair of shoes. That's when I decided to start this business on the one-for-one model. So we started really small and the two hundred fifty became a thousand and then five thousand and then ten thousand, and now something that started out as extremely small has given over two million children a new pair of shoes. My advice is to find your dream and then start small.

Mycoskie's advice is profound but startling in its simplicity: start small. When he founded TOMS, he didn't set out to create an enormous shoe company that would be carried by national retail chains, he just began to take small steps. His natural giftedness as an entrepreneur and the strength of his idea propelled his business forward.

Business gurus call this approach "scaling." Rather than waiting until a dream is ready to explode, an idea can be launched in a small way and tested. That helps prove whether or not the idea has legs before major investments are made. It's one thing to tell someone your idea at a cocktail party; it's another to show the world that it works. Once the dreamer proves that the idea resonates, he or she can focus on growing the business.

My friend Charlie focuses on a ten-year business plan that requires massive investment dollars, staffing, a Web presence, and marketing materials. He could start small, but he can't see the first step for the finish line. He's placed proving his idea ahead of scaling it, and the result is paralysis.

More than sound business, Mycoskie's approach to realizing one's dream is less stressful. When we focus on the finish line—a ribbon-cutting ceremony or hiring employees—the vast distance and myriad obstacles can overwhelm us. But if we consider only the first step, the idea seems more manageable. This way of thinking gives us freedom to move and flex and breathe.

If you're nurturing a dream and can't seem to realize it, let Mycoskie's advice guide you. Not every detail has to be resolved in order to get going. Start now, and start small. Slip on your shoes, and take the first step.

eight: Feedback

Jack Dorsey
Cofounder of Twitter and Founder of Square

My friend Derek settled in a medium-sized midwestern city after college because his new wife's family was there and he sensed that opportunities awaited him there. A natural entrepreneur, he entered the working world with unbridled zeal. Doors began opening for him with regularity.

One day, a big idea began germinating inside him: he wanted to start an organization built around an annual conference for young leaders. His vision was so strong that he ran into the endeavor headlong, without asking advice of experts, his friends, or others with similar organizations. By the time I learned of his plans, he had already passed the point of no return. He had filed the papers, picked a date, booked a venue, and launched a website.

Had my friend asked for my advice early on, I would have offered him one word: wait. The idea had legs, but it wasn't ready and neither was Derek. He needed time to expand his platform and to build a community large enough to sustain the organization. He needed to build trust and confidence around his brand before asking people to spend hundreds of dollars to support it. The idea needed to be tested before it was launched. Unfortunately, he took none of these steps.

Derek worked overtime to gather a small cadre of sponsors, exhibitors, and speakers. The attendance numbers crept up slowly while the conference date rushed toward him head-on. When the big day finally arrived, the event fell flat. Only a fraction of the attendees Derek had promised to sponsors showed up for the event. The venue he had rented was far too large and sucked all the energy out of the room. Participants and vendors left with a sour taste in their mouths, and Derek's credibility was obliterated. The organization folded under outstanding debts less than two years after its inception.

Looking back, Derek recognizes that he made a lot of the same mistakes other entrepreneurs have made—ones that could have been avoided had he sought the advice of others. His vision exceeded his capacity, and he adopted a ready-fire-aim approach, failing to do the necessary preparation. The idea was launched before it was tested, and he failed to gather feedback to refine it.

Like many who share Derek's insatiable entrepreneurial spirit, I have launched ideas before they were vetted. I am reminded that *entrepreneur* is French for "excitable." If we can hold our emotions in check long enough to run our ideas through credible filters, we can often avoid unnecessary failure and frustration.

Derek took the opposite approach from the one Jack Dorsey has adopted. Dorsey is the cofounder of Twitter and founder and CEO of Square, a mobile payments company. Twitter helped launch the revolution in Egypt and the Arab Spring, and Square is revolutionizing financial transactions. People are now paying their babysitters with their credit cards through a simple plug-in for their iPhones. Dorsey's careful planning has resulted in the creation of two business icons and landed him on the prestigious list of *Time*'s 100 Most Influential People. His net worth is estimated at more than $330 million, and he is only in his midthirties. When I sat down with him, I wanted to know what role feedback and testing played in his business endeavors.

KC: How important is feedback to you and your process of testing an idea as you move it to completion?

JD: I found myself early, early on thinking about what I could build. I would think, "If only I had this technology" or "If only I had this person to work with" or "If only this macro event was happening in the world, then I could really do this." But then I realized I was making excuses not to work on it. So I found that if I drew it up and got it out of my head, I could start criticizing it from a third-party perspective. I could start seeing it outside of my own head, and I think that's really, really important.

The second most important thing is to take the idea to a friend or a colleague or a family member and say, "Look, this is an idea I have, I think it's pretty interesting. What do you think?" Or even better, to actually program or create something and then show the friends or colleagues how they can use it or immediately get value out of it. You need to see their different perspective and way of thinking, and you can react to it defensively or you can allow it to be an inspiration.

I learned how to treat it more as an inspiration, as a way to drive the product forward. The biggest thing feedback does is allow you to have a moment where you can express what you are thinking, why you are thinking about it, and you can make a decision as to whether you should commit yourself or move on. And moving on doesn't mean forgetting about that idea, it means putting it on the shelf for now and maybe it emerges in another way or another time in your life.

Dorsey stressed the importance of seeking wise counsel before launching a new endeavor, not just after. No one would consider writing a book without a copy editor or releasing a drug without lab trials. Yet in the business world, many people attempt to live in a vacuum without the feedback of others.

In life, every person stares into a mirror at him- or herself. When we try to self-assess, it is almost impossible to get the full perspective. There is always a part of you that is doing the analysis, which is beyond evaluation. You cannot completely self-evaluate; everyone needs a third-party perspective in the development, launch, growth, and sustainability phases of his or her endeavors. Though we might assume that this would slow the process of innovation, Dorsey observes that it can actually propel the product forward.

But not all advice is created equal. There is good feedback and bad feedback. Sometimes you will be tempted to listen to the pessimism or poor perspective of a single individual that will divert you down a path you should not walk. When you are on the right path and doing what you're meant to, and a naysayer hits you at the wrong time with the wrong words, the range of feedback you've gotten will stabilize you and keep you from getting sidetracked by an outlying opinion. I've had various people say, "Ken, you can't do this," but their comments are placed in perspective by the many more who've said, "Ken, you're gifted and prepared for this." The way to protect yourself from bad feedback is to get comments from numerous sources. When you fill your bucket with a range of opinions, you'll have a better understanding of what reality looks like.

Consider the source as well. If you want good evaluation, you need feedback from people who will be brutally honest with you. The wrong *who* will give you the wrong *what*. Such an exercise is admittedly difficult because it means being vulnerable, exposing yourself, making a door in the walls you've built.

If an organization is an automobile, hard work is gasoline. But feedback helps you build a better car. In Derek's case, he filled up and cranked a car that was sitting on cinder blocks. If he'd carefully tested the idea and spoken with others, he wouldn't have ensured his company's success, but he would have increased its chances. Whether you are looking to launch a new idea or spearhead a project at your current company, open yourself to the wisdom of others. When you finally shift from park to drive, you'll find yourself better equipped for the hazards of the journey.

nine: Courage

John McCain
U.S. Senator (R—Ariz.) and Former Presidential Candidate

On the evening of June 5, 1989, I sat on the living room floor, leaning against the couch and furiously attempting to finish my homework before dinnertime. Dad sat next to me in a recliner, watching the nightly news. My fourteen-year-old fingers scratched the surface of college-ruled paper with a dull number two pencil. Following a commercial break, Peter Jennings appeared on the screen with his characteristic serenity, but the look in his eyes betrayed the big news he was about to deliver: the Chinese military had opened fire on unarmed protestors—mostly students—in Beijing who were calling for the Communist government to consider democratic reforms. Jennings recounted the violence in a careful cadence, and then the footage rolled.

A column of Chinese Type 59 tanks pushed through Tiananmen Square as a lone rebel stood directly in their path. The lead tank inched right in an attempt to drive around him, but the man countered the maneuver. The death machine lurched left, and the protestor stepped in front again. My pencil now hung loosely in the crux of my hand, and my eyes remained fixed upon the television set as that brave soul stared into the business end of a tank turret. He was daring the machine to run him over. The tanks ground to a halt as the demonstrator, who would be later known as "Tank Man," climbed atop the machine and attempted to communicate with the driver. Moments later, the man was dragged away, never to be identified.

Tank Man's picture appeared in every major newspaper around the world, and *Time* named the protestor one of the hundred most important people of the century. The scene was singed into my memory and that of my entire generation. Though some considered the man's act pure lunacy, my teenage mind recognized it as an emblem of raw courage. While others had hidden in the shadows, one man had stood firm upon his convictions in broad daylight.

Nothing inspires human beings as much as the courage of great men and women. As Americans, we idolize figures such as Patrick Henry, Susan B. Anthony, and Martin Luther King, Jr. We're inspired by tales of valor in the Continental Congress and on Normandy's beaches during World War II. Those stories loom large in our minds as examples of how stalwart leaders with iron backbones can change the course of history.

John McCain must surely rank among the most courageous American figures of the modern era. The son and grandson of four-star admirals, McCain chose a life of service over a life of comfort. He entered the U.S. Navy in 1958 as a fighter pilot and nearly died in the 1967 fire aboard the USS *Forrestal* during the Vietnam War. Three months later, his plane was shot down over Hanoi. He was captured by the North Vietnamese and held in a POW camp, where he was severely tortured and beaten. After his release in 1973, he once again chose to serve his country. Since 1987, he has served as a U.S. senator from Arizona.

When I received an opportunity to speak with Senator McCain, I delivered a question on two topics he knew well: courage and conviction.

KC: Senator, you once said, "Courage is that rare moment of unity between conscience, fear, and action, when something deep within us strikes the flint of love, of honor, of duty, to make the spark that fires our resolve." The first noun you mention—conscience—sticks out to me. How important are convictions to living a courageous life?

JM: You noticed what deserves most emphasis, and that is conscience. When I was in prison in Vietnam, for about a year and a half of the five and a half years that I was in there, my father was the commander-in-chief of all U.S. forces in the Pacific. And of course, Vietnam fell under his command. So I was a very valuable prisoner of theirs. One day, to my surprise, I was taken up to the head of all the camps. He was very nice and pleasant to me, and he offered me the opportunity to leave prison early and return to the United States. They did this periodically with groups of three during the Vietnam conflict.

I was not in good health. There was really only one guy that I was in communication with because I was in solitary confinement. It was a bit of a dilemma because my physical condition was not very good. Now, our code of conduct also says that we go home by order of sick and injured, and then by order of capture in case of prisoner release. And so it made it a little ambiguous because I was pretty badly injured.

But I refused their offer, because my conscience would not allow me to leave that prison camp before the other men, even at the risk of my life. Whether I would recover from my injuries or not, my conscience would not allow me to leave when there were others who had been there as long as two years before I was. I knew that I could never—if I came home to the United States and left them there—look at myself in the mirror and shave in the morning. So it was my conscience that did not allow me to accept their offer of early release from prison. Now, I must tell you as a postscript, I am glad I had no idea that I would be there another four years.

One of the things that I was sure of was that once I had refused their offer of release, things were going to be very, very tough, and they were very, very tough. The worst treatment I received was right after that. So to young people, I think the moral of the story is that you must know the difference between right and wrong.

Another example that I could tell you about conscience is about the Vietnamese. Part of their effort to win the war was to get prisoners to make tapes of war crimes confessions. I was taken up one time and roughed up pretty badly, and they said they wanted me to make this tape confessing my crimes. The guy said, "No one will know, no one will know that it was you." And I looked at him, and I said, "Yeah, but I will know. I will know."

So when I have talked with young people, I have tried to say to them that sometimes you will be tempted to do things that you know are not right, and no one will know that you did it. But you will know. You will know.

Stories like McCain's inspire us because of both their rarity and their moxy. He was given a "get out of jail free" card from his captors, and he said no because of his loyalty to his compatriots. How many of us would have chosen the same path, placing our convictions above our lives?

> "The guy said, 'No one will know, no one will know that it was you.' And I looked at him, and I said, 'Yeah, but I will know. I will know.'"

McCain knew his non-negotiables. He knew what was not for sale. Do you? What are the things you will not retreat from, that you will not compromise? Have you written them down? One of the most powerful tools for compromise is rationalizing. You'd be well served to write down and vocalize your convictions so that when you're faced with a temptation to compromise, you'll have the power to resist.

You'll likely never find yourself in a prison camp in Ho Chi Minh City, but you will face moments when you are tempted to compromise your convictions. You may be a businessman who is faced with a lucrative opportunity that requires ethically ambiguous actions or a parent who is tempted to slack off on your duties to your children because you are tired or stressed. Perhaps you're a spouse who is tempted to pursue an inappropriate relationship with another person despite your commitment to another "till death do you part." If you do not act on the courage to live what you believe and do what is right, no one else may know. But you will know.

Regardless of your life stage, you will hear the rumble of retreat and the growl of compromise. But when the tanks of your life meet the tips of your toes, stand tall, stand tough, and stand true. Let the courage of your convictions spark the fires of your resolve.

ten: Hard Work

Malcolm Gladwell
New York Times Bestselling Author

I need to make a confession: I'm a huge fan of *American Idol*. My wife and I settle in each week to watch talented singers compete their guts out while wrestling with nerves and confidence and all the other things people experience while journeying toward their dreams. I'm a sucker for a race-to-the-finish-line competition, and letting fans help select the winner strikes me as less contrived than other reality television shows.

Like other *American Idol* fans, Stacy and I relish the first episodes. We enjoy the auditions' comedy and tears, expectation and suspense. Who can resist the rush of excitement when hopefuls in pursuit of their goals break through the audition door waving the coveted yellow ticket to Hollywood? Viewers enjoy those moments of discovery, like beholding a butterfly shaking off its cocoon, those moments when they realize they've just witnessed the birth of a star.

Before season one aired, television audiences had never beheld such a sight. Contestants without the slightest ability pranced around in front of the judges and gave singing a bad name. When the judges dared to inform the youngsters that they lacked vocal talent, a bewildered look surfaced on their faces. I remember watching a girl finish an audition only to hear Randy Jackson softly say, "Girl, I'm sorry. But that was just awful. Singing is just not for you." Without missing a beat, the young lady shot back, "Okay! I'll see you in the next city." His words hadn't fazed her. She couldn't process the possibility that perhaps her gifts lay elsewhere.

Her story is part of a troubling trend that extends well beyond the iconic television show. I call it "reality deprivation syndrome," but experts label it the Dunning-Kruger effect, which is to say, "A cognitive bias in which the unskilled suffer from illusory superiority, mistakenly rating their ability much higher than the average, while the highly skilled underrate their abilities."[1] Some people refuse to realize the extremity of their own inadequacies.

In the contemporary United States, this malady seems to afflict children more than anyone else. Our culture encourages us to tell our children how great they are at every chance that presents itself. We remind them that they're special or even better than others. When they fail, we blame the teacher or the judges or the system, not allowing for the possibility that our children have suddenly discovered their own limitations.

If you observe an early episode in a season of *American Idol*, you'll notice the way parents are contributing to their child's delusions. Young contestants walk into the room thinking that they're the next Celine Dion or Michael Jackson, but viewers can see the train wreck before the engine leaves the station. In their interviews, the children talk about how badly they want to succeed and how much they believe in their talents. But then they open their mouths, and the sound of a dying farm animal fills homes across the United States. The contestants leave in tears, often falling into the arms of their parents, who are equally shell-shocked. The producers allow those awkward moments to air because it makes for delicious television, but I wish they'd drag the parents before the judges' table. Oftentimes the problem in these children's psyche isn't their own fault: it's a product of their enabling parents.

But society must also bear the responsibility. My wife and I grabbed a copy of a popular parenting magazine from our mailbox the other day, only to be confronted by a headline that screamed, "Raise the Next Steve Jobs." With that type of message, no wonder parents think that their kids—no matter their actual talents, potential, or commitment to work hard—are destined to become the next rock star, president, or world-changing innovator.

We parents spend so much time trying to make our kids *feel* good that we miss opportunities to teach them how long it takes to *be* good. The difference is a big one. If we spend our whole lives trying to make our kids feel good, they enter the world unaware of their true gifts. Later in life, when a college professor, coworker, or boss doesn't tell them they are good, they have nothing to fall back on. Why? Because they lack a framework for how to become good within their unique gift set.

> We parents spend so much time trying to make our kids *feel* good that we miss opportunities to teach them how long it takes to *be* good.

As a staff writer for *The New Yorker*, Malcolm Gladwell has explored the fringes of social psychology and penned four *New York Times* bestsellers. His book *The Tipping Point: How Little Things Make a Big Difference* has shaped the language used in boardrooms around the world. When I had the opportunity to ask him a single question, I decided to ask him how society can combat this troubling trend, beginning with parents.

KC: Overnight success is creating an epidemic of expectation among young people such that hard work is often undervalued. How can parents fight that notion?

MG: Parents have traditionally stressed the importance of things like music and sports as appropriate activities for young people. Far more important than a specific skill and a pleasure that come from those two things is the lesson that you learn, which is that no one who ever played an instrument or a sport can escape the conclusion that you are only as good as how hard you work. You cannot believe in the notion of instant celebrity or instant success or instant expertise if you have ever tried to play the piano or hit a baseball or run a mile, or do any of the things that people do in those two domains. So we have to counteract the messages we are getting from popular culture with the real lessons that you get from these kinds of disciplines.

With his characteristic cocktail of simplicity and profundity, Gladwell recognizes the lessons inherent when parents encourage their children to play a sport or learn an instrument. Those arenas are laboratories where limitations manifest themselves almost immediately. Kids learn something when they try to dunk a basketball and realize they can't. They discover something when they try to blow a trumpet and it makes their ears hurt. But those spaces also make room for probing their true talents and the role of hard work in developing them.

Our kids don't need us to emphasize their own inadequacies, and parents who constantly highlight their children's shortcomings are as dangerous as those who perpetually proclaim their superiority. The limits of each human being will be naturally discovered in places where the child is tested. I don't tell my son Ty that he's the best player on the soccer team. He knows he isn't the best, and I don't want that for him anyway; I want him to be the best he can be. Not the best person in every room, on every field, in every audition but *his* best.

Parents want their children to join them in believing that their kids are the best at everything. And as the psychologist William James told us, "There is nothing so absurd that it cannot be believed as truth if repeated often enough." Kids are incredibly perceptive. They innately know they aren't the greatest soccer player or cellist the world has ever seen. But when parents buck reality and tell them they are, they come to believe it.

Unfortunately, failure comes to us all. One day when the children fall flat on their faces and are forced to confront reality, their minds wander back to their first intuitions, and they recognize that Mom and Dad were lying to them the whole time.

But perhaps you are the coddled, not the coddler. You've grown up drunk on your own superiority, and, due to an unforeseen failure, you now recognize the need to recalibrate your honesty meter. Consider this an invitation to reality. Surround yourself with truth tellers, people who will help you stare deeply into an uncracked mirror. Be warned that you may feel a shock when you see the warts and scars and wrinkles that you didn't know existed. But you'll finally be free, for now you're dealing with reality as it exists and not as you might wish it to be.

When we plant our feet in reality's soil, we can discover our passions and gifts and begin working hard to develop them. That's where the magic happens. Only when you see yourself as you really are, can you begin to shape the person you'd like to be, and only when you recognize the valley in which you stand, can you map out the mountain you'd like to climb.

eleven: The Now

Andy Stanley
Pastor and Bestselling Author

Leadership gurus talk much about the future. From casting vision to setting goals to capitalizing on opportunities for advancement, there is no shortage of material about realizing your dreams for tomorrow. We swim in a sea of books and podcasts and tweets about the future, but I often find myself treading water and wondering "What about today?"

A longtime friend whom I'd lost touch with phoned me recently. I filled with excitement at the prospect of reconnecting, but when I answered his call, I realized that he needed me only to help close a business deal. Reluctantly, I offered my help. When I had done what he needed me to do, however, he vanished. No returned phone calls. No email replies. No handwritten thank-you card. The illusion of our friendship shattered under the weight of his ambition. He was racing toward his dreams, and he didn't have time for anyone who wasn't pushing him closer to the finish line.

A few days later, my friend Sharon had some amazing wins in her organization. Her team had been working on a lucrative deal for several months, and the company's future depended on their success. I had been helping her with some of the negotiations, and I called to congratulate her when the news broke that the deal had closed. Less than a minute into the call, she noted a few things we could have done more efficiently and then began strategizing about the next deal she was working on. She sent no emails congratulating her team on the win, and no one threw a celebration dinner. No one was rounded up and patted on the back. Instead, the office returned to business as usual.

The previous months seemingly ceased to exist, and the team felt dejected. You could feel souls throughout the organization sinking. Their leader was so myopically focused on the next deal that she couldn't celebrate their recent success.

I've realized that failure to fully live in the now is a problem for many leaders. Though it may seem a minor detail, the ripple effects are substantial. Employees begin to wonder if what they are doing actually matters. They stop believing in the company's mission. Turnover increases, morale decreases, and the organization's impact wanes. The leader, without even realizing it, is hacking away at the base of the organizational totem pole. The structure is weakened, and the trunk begins to teeter. Worse still, the leader's friends and family can begin to feel like commodities rather than comrades and confidants. Your wife grows distant, your children cry out for attention, and even your longtime friends seek intimacy elsewhere.

With those two events fresh in my memory, a question about living in the present percolated in my mind. I decided to seek out a pastor rather than a business guru because I wanted wisdom that cuts to the heart of the issue. Andy Stanley is the senior pastor of North Point Community Church, one of the United States' largest congregations. His books include *Creating Community*, *Enemies of the Heart*, and *How Good Is Good Enough?* His ministry and communication style are marked by a clear application of timeless truth. When I had the opportunity to ask him one question, he did not disappoint.

KC: Leaders who love progress inevitably face the temptation to obsess about the future and miss out on the present. How can one fully live in the now while keeping his eye on what's next?

AS: The first thing I do is acknowledge that this is a *tension to manage* and not a *problem to solve*. Leaders want to solve problems, make progress, and plan for the future, so it's important to recognize that this tension will never go away. That being said, I do some things that have helped keep me in the now.

First, I have a *written* description of my preferred future and my vision. It's one thing to "think" about them and "dream" about them, but writing them down results in a more complete and accurate picture. I can easily be caught up in *What's next?* and forget how important it is to make decisions in the *present* that will facilitate my preferred *future*. The written description helps me avoid that trap.

Most of my goals, as are most leaders' I've met, deal with measurable quantities: church growth, professional development, progress in business, but that is an incomplete picture of where I want to end up. Even if I achieve all of my goals in those areas, if I arrive in the future without healthy *relationships* with the people I love, I will have failed. But it's hard, if not impossible, to measure relationships. So I need a written picture . . . a visualization . . . to remind me.

My second point might seem obvious, but I need to say it. We need to take care of our physical bodies now or our futures won't matter. Nobody has a professional future without a healthy physical body; nobody has a spiritual ministry without a healthy physical body. The repercussions of ignoring your health will play out in all the arenas of your life.

Third, something I can do *in the present* is pay attention to my emotional "gauges." Some people are naturally good at this, and other people have to learn to do it. I have to ask myself if I am behaving in a way *now* that will ensure I have healthy relationships *later*. I also have to learn to pay attention to the emotional gauges of the people I love. When I write a description of my preferred future, the people I love are in there. So to arrive at a marketplace goal or a professional goal without the people I love, as I said before, I would consider failure. In the day-to-day grind, the day-to-day hustle and bustle, I am going to lean into the things that I can count so I need to pay special attention to my relationships. I need to check the "gauges."

Fourth, one critical thing I do is pay attention to the questions and comments of the people closest to me. I am not talking about family; I am talking about professional relationships. I think I am surrounded by people who will be honest with me, but sometimes that is difficult to monitor. If I develop the habit of paying attention to the questions I am most frequently asked and the comments that are most frequently made by those who are closest to me, I will become aware of the current health of my surroundings.

When people find themselves in trouble, there were usually warning signs . . . red flags waving. People were trying to point out things that could undermine their effectiveness. So pay attention to the questions and the comments of the people who are closest to you.

> **"I think every leader needs to get into the habit of asking: why am I doing what I'm doing?"**

I'd put the last point into the form of a question. I think every leader needs to get into the habit of asking: *why am I doing what I'm doing?* We are good at deceiving ourselves, at ignoring the ugly parts, the squiggly things under the rocks. So before I make a decision, whether it's relational, financial, or professional, I stop and ask this question. The answer ties me to my present circumstances even as I think about the future. If I am honest with myself, it will help me to fully live in the now while keeping my eye on what's next.

Stanley addresses the problem holistically, but he begins by asking us to grab a pen and some paper. As we write down our vision of the future, we are able to release it. We can post it on the wall and begin living in today. That sets us free from the tyranny of tomorrow, but it also reminds us of our current locale. If we aren't aware of where we are, we miss opportunities to make an impact. We fail to build energy among our team, forget to celebrate wins, and don't nurture our children or love our spouses. We become like a coach who says, "I want to be the greatest coach who's ever lived" but is so focused on his legacy that he fails to win the next game. Write down your vision, and then root yourself in the here and now.

Otherwise, we become like a child who stands in the midst of his birthday party with glazed eyes, dreaming about next year's birthday cake. Such a posture will emotionally bankrupt us. Though we might maintain the respect of our colleagues, our friends and partners will begin to feel like nothing more than objects and assets that will help us reach our next goal. We all know someone like that. They are the people in your life who are so transactional that you hear from them only when they need you. You spend hours and days and months in close proximity to them and never feel an inch closer. They rarely show gratitude to those around them, and when they do, it feels thin and rote.

To guard against this, Stanley says, we must remain connected to those around us. One of the greatest dangers for leaders is isolation. I call such people "Kentucky Derby leaders." A horse in that famous race may bump into the steeds running alongside of him, but its blinders keep it from ever seeing the other horses. It can see only the finish line or the horses in front of it. Others see us more clearly than we do, and they can help objectively assess if we've adopted unhealthy habits in pursuit of our goals.

So open your ears and begin listening to those around you. Seek out their opinions and assessments with your defenses low and your heart open. When you do, you will identify opportunities for growth, progress, and deeper relationships. And you will unleash the great irony of being present in the moment: that by taking steps to live in the now, we move closer to the goals we've set for the future.

twelve: Risk

Jim Collins
New York Times Bestselling Author

I looked up to Mike as one might a superhero, though he never knew it. We first met in college, and I wondered at his magnetic charisma. He dressed like a *GQ* model, and girls swooned as he cruised past them in the halls. He received a full scholarship due to his tremendous brainpower, a force he seemed to employ with little effort. He hailed from a wealthy family, drove a killer black BMW, and communicated with the precision of a long-standing senator. Years before Twitter, Mike was racking up followers everywhere he went.

Mike and I would often talk about our dreams and aspirations while visiting the library or waiting in line at the cafeteria. He said he might go into business or maybe politics. I knew he'd be successful in either field. If colleges had superlatives, Mike would have been a shoo-in for "most likely to succeed."

We lost touch after graduation, and for the next few years I scanned the magazine racks, searching for his face on the cover of *Forbes* or *BusinessWeek*. The surprise never came. Not that particular one, at least. While reconnecting with a mutual friend nearly a decade later, I discovered that his life had gone in a direction no one would have imagined.

You won't find Mike in any of America's great boardrooms today. If you wanted to meet him, you'd have to travel to Coco Beach, Florida. He'd greet you with a quick hello before rushing out with his long board to catch a few waves. He picks up work when he can, but he never takes on so much that it prevents him from surfing most days. When I asked where he lives today, I was shocked to hear him talk about switching between his car and his friends' apartments. The super-hero I once thought would conquer the world ended up a beach bum.

If you sat with Mike today, you'd find that he is still bursting with good ideas, but he never pursues them. Once shared, they go into the attic of his mind, where they collect dust. He dreams like Steve Jobs but executes like a blind man on an assembly line. He is the living embodiment of unrealized potential.

We all know a Mike. You've seen him in a thousand faces with a hundred names. Mike is your thirty-seven-year-old child who still lives in your basement and has little ambition outside of playing video games. The high school valedictorian you once admired who dropped out of college and now can't seem to hold down a job is a Mike. The spirit of Mike lives in your friend who displays exceptional creativity or intelligence but wanders aimlessly through life without ambition.

Viewed from the outside, those people have everything going for them. They're well liked, graduate at the top of the class, and have an exceptional network. The years pass, and they blow everyone away— not by how much they achieve but by how little. What happened? Why didn't they ever rise to the level of their ability?

If anyone could answer those questions, I figured it was Jim Collins. The *New York Times* bestselling author of books including *Good to Great, How the Mighty Fall,* and *Great by Choice,* Collins has studied the science of advancement as much as anyone. When I had the opportunity to ask him one question, I wanted to know why people like Mike seem destined for greatness but settle for mediocrity.

KC: Ambitious people and the way they tick fascinate me. I am equally curious as to why so many people lead average lives. Why do so many people never make the choice to pursue greatness?

JC: When I taught entrepreneurship and small business at Stanford Business School a number of years ago, I was always challenging my students to go out and carve a great path for themselves. I think there are two ways to approach life. You can try to do a paint-by-numbers kit, which means that you stay within the lines and end up with a nice picture, but you're not going to have a masterpiece. The only way to have a masterpiece is to ultimately try to paint a masterpiece on a blank canvas, your canvas.

I would challenge my students on this idea of not doing a paint-by-numbers approach to life but to go out and try to paint a masterpiece. Don't just try to have an entrepreneurial company, try to build a great company from the ground up because it's worthy to build something great for its own sake. Why did Beethoven make the Fifth Symphony so great? Because he could. I mean in the end, that's the answer.

I remember one conversation where a guy came to me and said, "I really heard what you said in the class, and I wanted to think about starting a company or doing something on my own. But I decided I'm too risk-averse, so I've decided to take a job with a large, established company."

I said, "Well, you just took on a lot of risk. You were telling me you are risk-averse. Let me ask you a question. What's the first thing you learn in finance? It's 'Don't put all your eggs in one basket.' What is a job with a large company that somebody else owns and runs? It's all your eggs in one basket held by somebody else, and if he mismanages it, he drops your eggs. That's a very risky strategy, it seems to me. You're not in control, and the political forces can get you. Why, if you were risk-averse, would you take a job like that?"

My students were not risk-averse, they were actually taking on more risk. In a number of cases they went to work for large, seemingly stable companies that were poorly managed and ended up going through economic calamity. All of a sudden they were blown out of the water by a political or economic shake-up and lost their job and twelve years working there. That's risky.

People are not risk-averse, they're ambiguity-averse. What really scares people is not the risk, it's the blank canvas. It's the ambiguity of carving our own path, trying to do something truly distinctive that is inherently unnerving to many of us. If you go and do something on your own, what do you do tomorrow? There is no set timeline, there's no sense of what's going to come next or how you're going to do it or what things are going to look like the next month or the month after. It's very, very ambiguous. It's opaque. It's the blank canvas. I've come to the conclusion that it's not that people are risk-averse, they are averse to ambiguity.

What most people attribute to risk aversion, Collins says, is actually due to fear of uncertainty. Individuals who suffer from it would rather live in the security of the mundane than launch out into a more promising, more ambiguous future. By choosing not to leap, they fail to achieve what might be possible otherwise, but at least they know their daily schedule and bank account balance and occupational trajectory. They are Linus, content to drag the security blanket of a humdrum life.

Outward appearances may seem to indicate that people like Mike are happy, but deep down, they aren't. As I've corresponded with Mike in the years since we reconnected, I sense that he is as perplexed by the direction his life has taken as I am. He traded the unknown for the predictable, but he received a heavy helping of discontent along with it.

But we must not be too hard on the Mikes in our lives, for there is at least a little Mike in us all. All of us have stood paralyzed at the end of a diving board while we wondered what lies just beneath the water's surface. Who among us is not afraid of the unknown? Who has never balked at making a decision because of an uncertain outcome?

Life's most profound lessons are captured along the uncharted path, but those who never walk it miss out.

Collins reminds us that what scares us most is the blank canvas, but he offers a bold challenge to pick up our brushes and start painting. You don't know how long it might take, what hurdles you may encounter, which sacrifices will need to be made, how many setbacks you'll experience, or how pleasing the portrait will look once you finish it. But we'll never know any of those things unless we lift our brushes and begin.

The real tragedy for the Mikes of this world is not failure to achieve but rather failure to learn. Life's most profound lessons are captured along the uncharted path, but those who never walk it miss out. As we forsake uncertainty and pursue our greatest passions, we begin to realize that we're learning about life, others, and ourselves along the way. When an artist lays his brush down for the final time, he often realizes that the act of painting is as beautiful as the masterpiece itself. So to every Mike in the world and even the one inside us all: pick up your brush, and start painting.

SURVIVING

thirteen: Failure

Pat Summitt
Hall of Fame Coach of the Tennessee Lady Vols Basketball Team

I was a senior point guard at a small private school when a defining moment happened to me. The number-four-ranked high school basketball team in Virginia was coming to our gym. They were better than we were, and both teams knew it. This game was our shot at taking down the giant, and Benny Polk, my wire-thin, spitfire coach relentlessly prepared us for the game.

We were ready. For four quarters, we gave everything we had. We played the game of our lives, and with four minutes left, we scored to get within one point. Our small gym was packed to the rafters, and the crowd noise was deafening. Our scrappy, undermanned squad had played to the level of a great team, and we could taste victory.

The opposing coach played a wild card: when his team brought the ball past half court, he instructed them to hold it. There is no shot clock in high school basketball, so they could have held the ball until the game ended if we had let them. Coach Polk realized what was going on and decided to hold us back and let the clock run. The chess game was on. For three minutes, both teams stood and watched the clock while glancing at the coaches for a signal.

With a minute to go, Coach Polk instructed us to press. Our defense made the stop, and we regained the ball with twenty seconds left on the clock. After a time-out, we came back onto the court with a play designed to give us the last shot and a chance to pull off a stunning upset. We inbounded the ball and ran the play. It worked. The shot was open, and my teammate David Weddell released it.

When the ball left David's hands, time slowed and gravity ceased. The ball hit the inside of the rim and bounced out. The buzzer sounded, the game ended, and we had lost.

Whether you're an athlete or not, you know the feeling. You worked to please your spouse for fifteen years, but he left you for a younger woman. When everyone else left early, you put in overtime at the office, and somehow you ended up on the chopping block. Your team played its guts out, but the ball didn't drop. Now you're defeated, depressed, discouraged. It doesn't matter who you are, where you live, what career path you've chosen, or how bad your "luck" is, everyone has experienced failure and loss.

Even Pat Summitt, the all-time winningest coach in NCAA basketball history, lost her share of barn burners. She was a master of the 4,700 square feet of roundball real estate who amassed eight NCAA Championships, twenty-nine combined Southeastern Conference Championships, and well over a thousand regular season wins. But at the time of her retirement, she'd still amassed 208 heartbreaking losses.

The secret to Pat's success is that even when a loss crushed her, it never crippled her. She was always able to pick up the pieces of her team and keep pressing forward. Shortly after I had the privilege of interviewing the legendary lioness, she announced to the world that at the age of fifty-nine she was taking on the fiercest competitor she had ever faced: early-onset dementia and Alzheimer's disease. For nearly four decades, the coach had kept the Lady Volunteer basketball program among the nation's elite and, in the process, changed the way women's collegiate hoops were perceived across the country. When I sat down with her, I didn't ask how she had managed to acquire a mammoth number of victories. I wanted to know how she had responded to defeats.

KC: What is one of the most valuable lessons you have learned from failure?

PS: My first loss as a coach was against Mercer University. I was just overwhelmed and had tunnel vision. The only individuals I could see were our players. I could not tell you what Mercer was running on offense or defense, and I knew after the game that I just didn't do a good job.

I remember calling home, and my mother answered the phone, and I asked if my dad was there. She said yes and handed him the phone. My dad did not like to talk on the phone much. He said, "All right?" Well, I was so nervous because I knew how competitive he was. I said, "Hey, Dad." He then said, "Did you win?" And I said, "No, sir, we lost."

Long pause. I didn't know what he was going to say other than "You need to get out of coaching." But he said, "So you lost?" I said, "Yes, sir." I will never forget what he said next. He said, "Let me tell you one thing. You don't take donkeys to the Kentucky Derby. You better go get you some racehorses."

And then he hung up. I knew what he was saying to me, and it really shaped me in terms of my philosophy to understand that you win in life with people. It was not about me. I have never scored a basket for the University of Tennessee. Winning is all about the people you surround yourself with and what they bring to the game, to the office, to life.

> **"Winning is all about the people you surround yourself with and what they bring to the game, to the office, to life."**

"You don't take donkeys to the Kentucky Derby." That simple but profound homespun wisdom forever altered the mind-set of the one of the greatest coaches ever to wear a whistle. *People matter.* Great people are the difference makers. If you are leading a team at any level, in any field, this nugget of wisdom is all you need to know about building a successful team.

Even more amazing than that lesson is the realization that Summitt might not have learned it. Had she lain in bed that week with the curtains drawn, refusing to take phone calls, she might not have achieved so much. But she knew if you want to know how to get to the top in life, you had better learn from what drives you to the bottom.

When people are consistently successful for a long period of time, we tend to assume that they have always been on top. I have interviewed many great people and champions over the last few years, and I have always been more impressed with how they handled failure than with how they managed to succeed. To a person, they have all learned more from failure and setbacks than from any of their mountaintop moments.

I'll never forget the night we lost that epic game my senior year in high school. My team sobbed for what seemed like a week in the locker room, and no one could even talk. We couldn't process what had just happened. When he caught his breath and gathered his thoughts, Coach Polk finally spoke. "I am so proud of this team. You left your hearts on the floor tonight and played like champions. I know it hurts, but get your chins up," he said, his voice quavering with emotion. "Don't let this loss define our season."

His words didn't take away the pain, but they did teach me something that has guided me on the journey of life. In that moment of despair, I realized that sometimes you can play your very best and still lose. You can do your very best and still get passed over. But it's how you respond to those losses that matters. The right response to failure doesn't mean your soul won't ache as you languish in life's locker room, but it will allow you to hold your head high when you walk back out on the court. As Pat Summitt's life and career clearly illustrate, every great winner is also a great loser.

fourteen: Fear

Michael Hyatt
New York Times Bestselling Author and Chairman
of Thomas Nelson Publishers

The name Walt Disney World conjures up words such as "wonder" and "imagination." For most people, the renowned theme park's moniker rarely summons up bone-rattling, tear-inducing fear. But my son Ty had a different experience during a recent family vacation to Disney's Animal Kingdom.

From the moment we stepped onto the property, my family was met with all the pageantry for which Disney is famous. The 500-acre amusement park is home to 1,700 exotic animals. Iguanas sunbathe on rocks, giraffes strut along savannas, and macaws showcase their neon feathers from perches just beyond one's fingertips. From the fanciful to the mighty, this Floridian wonderland is a kid's dream.

As with other Disney properties, the directory located near the entrance is dotted with attractions. Only a few steps in, a particular marker caught Ty's attention: Kali River Rapids. Contrary to its threatening name, the water ride is an opportunity for weary parents to put up their feet and exhale. A twelve-passenger circular raft winds down a picturesque river with jasmine-scented mists and majestic waterfalls. If you don't mind getting wet, this ride is not to be missed, and Ty made sure we wouldn't forget by reminding us about it every few steps we took.

Arriving at the entrance, I made sure my son met the height requirement, and we began the five-minute walk to the loading area. As we strode along, Ty's countenance changed from excitement to malaise to suspicion to outright anxiety. Stepping up to the turntable that places visitors in rafts, his emotional dam broke. Tears poured from his eyes as he pleaded passionately to leave. I knelt down and reasoned with him, something every dad attempts in such a situation even though he knows it's futile. I explained that the ride wouldn't scare him and that if he could just muster the courage to step into the boat, he'd be glad he did. A few minutes after launching into my monologue, we were trekking back to the attraction's entrance, serenaded by my son's relieved sniffles.

Just as we entered the common area, a second transformation happened. When Ty's little brother, Chase, proclaimed his desire to take on the rapids, Ty was suddenly convinced that he had made the wrong decision. He wanted to return to the Kali River Rapids turntable once more. My frustration over the whole ordeal had risen to boiling, but it was dwarfed by my own desire to experience the ride. So after a third five-minute walk, we were finally floating through the Asian-style jungle together.

I looked over at Ty after a few minutes and saw his characteristic smile, the one that never fails to melt me. He reached over, gripped my hand, and shouted, "Dad, I love it! It isn't scary at all . . . thanks!" Suddenly, I was the one who was being transformed—from the emotionally and physically drained father to the proud daddy. Despite the hassle of the ordeal, I knew Ty had experienced something profound, a lesson he could never receive through lectures or logic: he'd discovered how to conquer his fear.

The image of my smiling son was in the front of my mind when I drafted an interview question for Michael Hyatt. He is the chairman of Thomas Nelson Publishers, one of the largest book publishers in the United States. Highly respected among his peers and widely sought after for his leadership advice, Hyatt speaks often about how he's had to push through fear in order to achieve great accomplishments in his life. I wanted to know what his experiences could teach the rest of us who often find ourselves stopped dead in our tracks, begging to walk back the way we came.

KC: Many times in life, people don't go after what's on their hearts because of fear. How can we conquer fear?

MH: I think fear is the number one obstacle that most people face in their lives. Very few people talk about it, but I can guarantee you that it's the biggest thing that I face in my own heart. There have been times when I have lain awake at night wondering, particularly in this economy, "What's going to happen to me? What's going to happen to my company? What's going to happen to my family?" Fear is a very debilitating thing. It doesn't serve many useful purposes, and people can get really stuck in it.

When I'm afraid, I have a practice of walking right into my fears rather than away from them. If people can get used to that, their fear will dissipate. Most of the power of fear is in your mind; it doesn't really exist. It's just this idea that looms because we are unwilling to face it. But the way to declaw it, the way to defuse it, is to step into it—right into the middle of it—and do the thing that you are afraid to do.

How many times do we find ourselves frozen by fear? Our hearts palpitate, our eyes search frantically for an exit, and soon we're paralyzed by trepidation. At moments when we need to lunge forward, our feet plant as though in cement.

Fear takes many forms. I find myself arrested by the fear of criticism. I fear looking back on my life and discovering wasted opportunities or unrealized potential. A great worry for me is that I will have lived life but never made a difference. Maybe you are a perfectionist and battle the fear of

Fear lives mostly in our minds and festers as long as we fail to face it.

failure. Or you're shy and stave off the fear of success. Whatever brand of fear you experience, the emotion can be debilitating.

Hyatt is right; fear lives mostly in our minds and festers as long as we fail to face it. Children, for example, often convince themselves that something is under their bed. The fear may not be rational, but it can cause much distress. Yet the emotion remains only as long as the child lies motionless in the dark. Once he or she looks under the bed and finds nothing, the panic dissipates.

Likewise, Ty didn't have a real fear that memorable afternoon at Disney. I am his father, and he trusts me. He knows I wouldn't endanger him physically or emotionally. But he still felt afraid, and facing that emotion was the only way to chase it away. What my son learned as a six-year-old, many of us need to learn at twenty-six or fifty-six: that fear can protect us from danger—but it can also keep us from life's great adventures.

fifteen: Rejection

Soledad O'Brien

CNN News Anchor and Special Correspondent

Like many entrepreneurs, I'm always gazing at the horizon. I'm fixated on thoughts of what is next, what is coming, what may be possible. At thirty-four, I was overcome with a sense of restlessness. Having achieved a comfortable life in the business world, I could have set my life on cruise control and coasted for many years. But my eyes were searching for a sunrise.

I'd dreamed of working in radio for many years and figured that was as good a time as any to pursue it. I cold-called a large radio station in Atlanta and, through what must have been a miracle, secured a meeting with the program director. "Sam, I'm not here for any money, and I don't have unrealistic expectations," I said, not wanting to waste his time. "I am willing to do anything you need done, and I'll do it for free. Are you open to this?"

He let out a long breath as he sized me up. "You have a deal, Ken."

For the next six months, I worked at the station three days a week for several hours. I fetched coffee for hosts, conducted show research, and typed memos. Over time I made friends with several hosts, and they began putting me on the air to comment on recent sports happenings. I developed an idea for a segment called *Life Is Sport* that turned into a four-episode feature on Comcast Sports Southeast, a twelve-state regional television channel with more than ten million subscribers.

Everything was going well until I called the program director one day to request a press pass for a big story I was covering. Sam refused my request without explanation. I pressed him for an answer, and he combusted. "Ken, stop pushing me on this. You're not a company employee, so I can't give you a press pass. And you are not going to be on the air anymore!" he shouted. "You'll never make it in a number seven market. This is a huge market, and you need to move on."

I hung up the phone with my head spinning, fighting back rage. For more than half a year, I had worked for free, done more than what was asked of me, and attempted to deliver great content when I was allowed on the air. For no apparent reason and without explanation, everything I'd worked for was gone. And worse, a professional in the field had questioned my competency for the entire profession.

Looking back, I can't put my finger on why Sam discouraged me. Maybe he felt threatened or was projecting his own insecurities on me. Perhaps he was just power-tripping or having a bad day. Regardless, his words crushed my spirit.

Months later, I had the opportunity to interview Soledad O'Brien, the CNN anchor on the network's weekday morning show, *Starting Point*. As a strong woman and a child of immigrants—her father from Australia and her mother from Cuba—she's faced hurdles in her own career that required patience and perseverance. I wanted to get her perspective on how to handle situations like the one I'd faced.

KC: What would be your advice for young people who hear "no" when pursuing their dreams?

SO: I think the key is to not think of it as a "no," but as a "not here." I remember working in San Francisco, and a producer had said to me, "You know, you want to expand your skill set; you should learn how to anchor. Because one day something will happen—a plane will crash, the president will be shot—and you will have to sit in the chair and anchor a show, and you should have practice doing that. If you're going to be a reporter, you really should know how to anchor."

So I went to my boss at the station in San Francisco, and he said, "We have enough women anchors; we don't need any more." It became very clear that I was not going to grow there, and that was fine. Without any acrimony at all I said, "Okay, then I'm leaving."

And I went and got another job where I could have an opportunity to grow.

I always felt that my personal résumé was about growing and building my skill set, and the minute I ran into somebody who would say, "No, I think you can only be this," I would shift to moving around them. It was much in the same way as my parents did when I was a kid. When they were told they weren't allowed to get married because they were of different races, they drove to D.C. and got married because that's what they really wanted to do.

So "no" doesn't necessarily have the authority that I think sometimes young people feel. The first "no" can sometimes cause people to say, "That's it. I'm done. I've been told no." Sometimes that person saying no just has his own fear or he doesn't have an answer, and he's not going to say, "Well, I have no clue," so he says, "No." And if you dodge around that enough, you realize that a "no" doesn't necessarily have to stop you.

> **"I always felt that my personal résumé was about growing and building my skill set, and the minute I ran into somebody who would say, 'No, I think you can only be this,' I would shift to moving around them."**

Not only did O'Brien's opinions console me, they also fit squarely within my own experiences. The Saturday following that discouraging conversation with Sam, I was mowing my lawn and processing all that had transpired. (Yard work is my mental bio-dome.) As blades turned and grass clippings flew, I realized that one program director's "no" didn't have authority over me. Sam couldn't determine my career path; only I could do that. To persist, I didn't have to keep kicking a locked door; I needed to try a new one.

With a flash of fresh inspiration, an idea was born for creating a new resource called "One Question with Ken Coleman." Over the next few weeks, the idea grew and developed until the first segment went live online. More than 3,400 people visited my site that day, and the audio blog was rated by iTunes as a "New and Noteworthy Podcast." More interviews followed, more content was produced, and over time the project developed into the book you now hold in your hands.

O'Brien is right when she says, "A 'no' doesn't necessarily have to stop you." As you pursue your calling in life, you will experience rejection. Count on it. When you encounter hurdles and obstacles, don't let them deter you. Let them refine you, grow you, reinvigorate you. Sometimes you need to learn when to let go of a doorknob and move to another door.

In hindsight, I realize I needed that first opportunity to close in order to search for a new one, a better one, the right one. The program director's unnecessary insult turned out to be the very thing I needed to hear. A stop sign became a starting line, a dead end became a detour, and discouragement morphed into transformation. I now see the program director's "no" as one of my life's biggest "yes"es.

On January 7, 2012, I launched my own radio show with the thirty-ninth president of the United States, Jimmy Carter, as my first guest. Sam's words returned to my mind, and I smiled. His comments on the phone that day helped me realize my dream, and the rejection in your life can too.

sixteen: Criticism

Michele Bachmann
U.S. Congresswoman (R—Minn.)

Early in my interviewing days, I created a television segment called *Life Is Sport*. Each interview featured athletes, managers, and coaches highlighting how sports provided a space for them to learn real-life lessons. One afternoon, I decided to post online a segment with John Schuerholz, the president of the Atlanta Braves. No interview is perfect, but I was proud of that one.

A few hours after the video went live, I noticed a comment on the Web page that rattled me. A person whose name I didn't recognize was viciously criticizing the interview. He said I hadn't been paying attention and called my interview "lazy." The language was so hateful, I wondered if it was a joke. I deleted the comment with a quick click, but his words lingered in my mind.

For days, I carried that faceless person's words with me. I questioned my ability to pursue my calling. I fought embarrassment over the segment even though I hadn't been able to muster the courage to rewatch it. "Maybe he's right," I told myself.

On a slow afternoon a week later, I decided that either I could let his attack inflict pain on me or I could use it as a springboard for personal evaluation. That was the first time I received harsh criticism, but, like all professionals, I knew it wouldn't be the last. With my interview questions in hand, I played the interview back. Moments later, I realized that the interview really was as good as I thought it had been. But I still took time to note places where it could have been stronger.

Humans have never lived in a moment where so many people can be so visibly critical (or downright hateful) with so little risk of repercussion. Today, anyone can set up a blog, a Twitter account, or a Facebook group page and make all kinds of hurtful comments while hiding behind a wall of anonymity. Regardless of where it comes from, each time you receive criticism—whether in public or private—you can choose to either dwell on it or grow through it.

U.S. Congresswoman Michele Bachmann has learned that lesson only too well. In 2011, the woman representing Minnesota's Sixth District entered the Republican presidential primary race to the applause of many and even won the Iowa straw poll. But in January 2012, after finishing sixth in the Iowa caucuses, she dropped out of the race. Whether one aligns with her politics or not, no one can dispute that Representative Bachmann was the recipient of harsh critique. Liberal commentators often pummeled her, and late-night talk-show hosts caricatured her. I wanted to know how Bachmann views the sting of criticism.

KC: No matter who you are, critics are plenty and criticism hurts. What have you learned about managing the personal impact of criticism while moving forward on purpose?

"Criticism forced me to do a better job learning how to explain my position, why I came to the conclusions that I have, and really it has turned out to be a blessing in disguise."

MB: I have the advantage of being the only girl growing up in a family with three brothers, so that's a great preparation for politics. Also, I'm a conservative from a very liberal state, so I have been used to a lot of criticism from the media over the years. The criticism has forced me to be better. Criticism forced me to do a better job learning how to explain my position, why I came to the conclusions that I have, and really, it has turned out to be a blessing in disguise.

I came from a middle-class background, but then, like millions of other families, my parents were divorced. When that happened, we went to below poverty, literally overnight. My mom did the best she could, but at twelve or thirteen years of age, I had to start getting jobs babysitting just to be able to buy my clothing, my glasses, and my lunch at school. It taught me the value of a dollar, persistence, and hard work, all of which are great life lessons.

If there is anything that I've learned in life, it's that when criticism and suffering come your way, because they come to us all, we have two ways that we can react. We can either use suffering in our life to help us learn lessons and be better, or we can become bitter. That's why I encourage our children to take the route to become better; don't become bitter.

Despite our best efforts, we can't ignore criticism. But we can better cope with it if we know who we are and believe in what we're doing. Criticism often calcifies its victims, causing them to retrench. But if one remains teachable, words that seem a curse can become a great gift. "We can either use suffering in our life to help us learn lessons and be better, or we can become bitter," as Bachmann says.

Whenever I encounter criticism these days, I ask two questions. First, what in the words is true? Often criticism is like a peanut, wrapped in an inedible shell of anger but possessing a kernel of truth deep inside. We can learn from the true parts if we can identify them. Second, what in the words is beneficial? Often words are true but have no redeeming value. A personal attack on someone may be true, but there is no benefit in it; the criticism can't be learned from. Other times, there is a truth that can be acted upon.

People often preface statements by warning that they're about to offer "constructive criticism." As Representative Bachmann notes, what makes criticism truly constructive is your posture, not theirs. When we encounter this inescapable wart of life, the way we receive it will make all the difference. Rather than allow criticism to crush our spirits, we must use it as a springboard for improving the very element someone was attacking.

seventeen: Obstacles

Michelle Rhee
CEO of StudentsFirst and Former Chancellor of
D.C. Public Schools

I sat in my dentist's waiting room and stared outside at the overcast sky that's all too common on a December day in Georgia. My fingers rapped on the end table. I wondered how many more minutes would slip out of my life before the assistant would open the door and call my name.

My idle hands finally reached for a magazine, and I thumbed through all the usual suspects: *Cosmopolitan, Elle, People*. Why don't dentists ever seem to stock up on men's magazines? I wondered. From the corner of the table, a copy of *Time* caught my eye. A youngish Korean-American woman in a black pantsuit stood proudly before a chalkboard. Her hands gripped a broom, and a scowl decorated her face. The headline next to her read, "How to Fix America's Schools." Having children who were nearing their elementary school years, I decided to give it a read. What I discovered fascinated me.

Michelle Rhee took over as chancellor of Washington, D.C.'s, public school system in 2007 at a mere thirty-seven years old. At the time of her appointment, D.C. was struggling with one of the United States' worst school systems. When she arrived, less than half of ninth graders could expect to graduate in five years, and very few students were reading at grade level.[1] The district was 80 percent black, poverty-stricken, overstaffed, and inefficient. Rhee was hired to turn things around.

The young reformer arrived on the scene with both barrels blazing. Almost immediately, she announced that she would close 23 underused schools and restructure another 26. She fired 98 central-office employees, 24 principals, 22 assistant principals, 250 teachers, and 500 teaching aides. The Type A leader instituted a radical merit-based pay system for teachers and began investing the savings from her downsizing into technology upgrades.[2]

Few people disagree that the U.S. educational system needs work. Though we spend more money per child on education than most other developed countries do, our nation's students are behind most of them in math and science. But education reformers don't agree on how to make the necessary changes. Rhee enacted her reforms, but she faced massive opposition.

In a world where education is not just essential but indispensible, I recognize the importance of the quality of my children's learning experience. Though I can't rely on my kids' teachers to instill in them all they need to know, I realize that it is a big portion of their personal development. Even though I don't know exactly what ought to be done to improve the condition of our schools, I'm convinced that much needs to be accomplished.

Because Rhee bypassed traditional channels for changing the system, she was reviled by teachers' unions and battled with education lobbyists. Her opponents claimed she was a dictator who ran roughshod over anyone who got in her way, and they dubbed her executive staff the "Rhee-volutionaries." They decried her performance-based salary system, claiming that it failed to accurately answer the vexing questions of what makes a good teacher, and how do you measure it? Unfortunately for them, Rhee reported directly to the mayor. Not even the school board had authority over her.

The proof turned up in the pudding for Rhee. When she resigned as chancellor to found StudentsFirst, she turned over a school system that was in better shape than she had found it. The district now operates with leaner budgets and streamlined staffs and boasts higher test scores. She was named one of *Time's* 100 Most Influential People and became the hero of *Waiting for Superman*, a film that won the best documentary award at the 2010 Sundance Film Festival. Oprah Winfrey called Rhee a "warrior woman for our times."

The door finally swung open, and I heard my name called. As I walked into the back office, I admired Rhee's ability to overcome difficulties and make tough decisions. I was determined to interview her and ask one question on how to lead when others seem intent on shipwrecking you.

KC: Tough decisions are almost always met with obstacles, which can paralyze one's progress in life. What have you learned in your journey about leading in the face of obstacles?

MR: You know a very good friend and mentor of mine told me when I was at the beginning of my journey at DCPS, the D.C. public schools, that when you are leading you have to lead from the front. That means if you get too mired in the muck of things and get too concerned with how you are going to keep everyone happy and that sort of thing, then you lose sight of what's most important.

Sometimes you have to lead from the front in order to see some things that others can't. It's important to keep those things in mind and that way everyone will be available to eventually see those as well and come along afterward.

I think, for me, the most important thing is that you know you are making decisions for the right reasons. In my case, we believed very, very firmly that every decision we were making was in the best interest of the kids. Even though it's sort of difficult along the way, the benefit of making decisions for the right reasons does outweigh the challenges that you face along the way. And, so you know for me, it is about keeping the endgame in mind. Sometimes you need thick skin to do that.

> "I think, for me, the most important thing is that you know you are making decisions for the right reasons."

When Rhee reminds us that we must learn to lead out front, she speaks not of a physical position but of a mental posture. Influencers mustn't fixate on making everyone happy. Their eyes must be focused on the goal. Your gaze must fix upon what lies ahead rather than divert to the naysayers who encircle you. Your detractors won't likely be converted anyway. So if you try to please everyone, you often end up pleasing no one.

Rhee's example reminds me of a quote by the frontiersman Davy Crockett: "Be sure you're right, then go ahead." She echoes his sentiments when she says, "Even though it is very difficult along the way, if you're making decisions for the right reasons, it helps you face challenges." You can lead in uncertainty, but it helps to know that you're heading for moral high ground even as you recognize that the path you've chosen to get there is imperfect.

You may question whether what you're doing is best, you may debate whether your actions are most efficient, but you must believe that you're doing the right thing. If you commit to the right things and learn to lead from the front, you'll receive some of life's best education.

eighteen: Decisiveness

Patrick Lencioni
New York Times Bestselling Author

The first day of our family vacation was going surprisingly well. Not a single tear had fallen from any of our children's eyes. No temper tantrums had been thrown. And Stacy and I were having a great time with the friends who had driven down to Florida to join us. But when dinnertime arrived, the dynamic shifted.

While soaking up sun rays on the beach, we polled the children, who were too busy playing to be of any help, to tell us where they wanted to go to eat. Then the women asked the men, who responded with a unified "We don't care so long as they serve food." Finally, the women turned to each other and began a deliberation worthy of FBI hostage negotiators.

One of them picked up a dining brochure at the hotel's front desk, and together they combed out the establishments that were family-friendly. Then they began compiling reviews about each of the places on their smart phones, placing them into a hand-drawn table on the back of the brochure. Just when I thought they had selected a restaurant, a fellow sunbather leaned in to inform us of his bad experience there the previous evening. A pen crossed the name off the list, and discussion commenced again. The list began to grow rather than shrink, but our friend finally picked up the phone to make a reservation at the name topping her list. The hostess answered and informed her that no reservations were available before our children's bedtime. Another name was scratched from the list.

"Let's start from the beginning and make a pro and con list," our friend remarked.

Her words set off something deep inside me. I imagine it was the same feeling that overtakes Bruce Banner right before he transforms into the Incredible Hulk. My stomach began rumbling and growling, and then my chest started bouncing, and before I could stop it, a shout erupted from my mouth: "Will someone please just make a decision?"

My outburst represents a scenario that many people have faced in a social setting. Whether you are on a double date trying to pick a movie or tied up in a chain email where your extended family attempts to make plans for the holidays, participants throw out suggestions. The list of options grows. Pros and cons are batted around. And the can of decision keeps getting kicked down the road.

In such moments, you feel the same anxiety that everyone else does. You don't want to pick a movie that everyone hates, suggest a restaurant that no one likes, or have your idea shot down by the group. So you sit back and play the game like the others. Now everyone is following someone, but no one is leading anyone.

The tension that unfolds in such mundane moments also arises in significant settings. The fears and worries that plague us in the everyday also paralyze us in the once-in-a-lifetime. One of my childhood friends, Brian, has a ninety-two-year-old grandmother who is beginning to succumb to the trials of old age. She's a proud and independent matriarch who uses the Internet and even has a Facebook account. But her vision and hearing are slipping from her grasp. During the past year, she was involved in several fender benders while driving, and all of them were her fault. So the family gathered to discuss how they should intervene.

Her children and grandchildren sat in a circle throughout Brian's living room and discussed taking her car keys from her permanently. The decision was the right one, and most of the family knew it. Last year's minor accidents could become tomorrow's fatalities. Yet no one could pull the trigger because they wanted to respect her. The conversation got bogged down in the complexities and discomfort and risks of the decision until finally they decided to reconvene a month later. "Pop" goes the can as it tumbles down the road.

Those scenes illustrate a tendency many people struggle with: indecision. Too often in life, we choose delay, denial, or deliberation when what we need is decision.

Pat Lencioni is the founder and president of the Table Group, a management consulting firm that focuses on issues like this one. He has written nine bestselling books, including *The Five Dysfunctions of a Team*, with nearly three million copies sold. Organizations from Southwest Airlines to General Mills to Barnes & Noble have sought his advice on how to improve their organizational structures and decision-making processes. When I interviewed him recently, I wanted to ask him about the big, bad habit of indecision that afflicts so many people.

KC: Life is a never-ending onslaught of decisions, and they come in all sizes. Learning when and how to make the best decision is invaluable to reaching our full potential. How can we create a habit of decisiveness?

PL: I think the most important part of developing a habit of decisiveness is simply good old exposure therapy. Every time we make a decision, even when we are unsure, we learn that in most cases the decision works out well. When it doesn't, we still benefit because we learn and adjust accordingly. So the more times we're decisive in the face of uncertainty, the more we learn and the more comfortable we become.

Conversely, when we are indecisive, ambiguous, or hesitant, we often get frustrated with ourselves. Being decisive again and again helps us to realize that we survive no matter the outcome. So, as with anything else, if we want to get in the habit of something like exercise, for example, we need to go simply do it until it becomes second nature. Then the benefits become apparent.

I find that we place too much emphasis on what decisions we make rather than how we choose to execute on our decisions. In other words, people put too much emphasis on the decision sciences. We ask ourselves, Did I make the right decision? when the real question should be, How well did I execute against my decision? If we evaluate our decisions on a ten-point scale, one being a bad decision, ten being a great decision, a person can make a level-seven decision and it still turns out better than someone who makes a level-ten decision if the level-seven person is better at execution. General Patton's famous quote says it all: "A good plan violently executed today is better than a perfect plan executed next week."

In our world today, people want to turn around and evaluate every decision they make in hindsight as to whether it was right. Think of the NFL draft. Teams tend to ask, Did we pick the right player? The question should be, Did we use that player well?

> **"I find that we place too much emphasis on what decisions we make rather than how we choose to execute on our decisions."**

Regardless, it's important to remember that good things happen when we are decisive. We need to realize that our ability to execute against the decisions we make is just as important, or more so, than the actual decision. And finally, it has been critical for me to come to terms with the fact that we don't have complete control over how things turn out. For me, I rely on my faith in God. When I trust that God has a plan for me that I might not understand, it takes away the sense that every decision needs to be perfect or that it is all up to me.

Lencioni says that executing on a decision is more important than which decision was made. In other words, we spend too much time deciding how to jump out of the boat when we need to focus on where to swim when we hit the water. Should you dive in or opt for a cannonball? It matters less than you'd assume. Choosing wrong will teach you an invaluable lesson that you'll be able to use next time you make the leap.

If you're a parent, the way you nurture your kids will be as important as the decision to have them. If you're a director of an advertising agency who chooses to purchase a Super Bowl ad, your biggest concern is not whether or not that was the best choice; it's creating the best Super Bowl ad you can. So get going; the mistakes you'll make along the way will provide you with valuable wisdom.

We all want progress, and we know that our decisions are the engines that move us forward. But we need to recognize that making a decision *is* progress. Because we realize the first truth and not the second, we often find ourselves frozen in decision limbo. Instead, we need to simply move forward. The other problem is that we obsess over making the right decision when sometimes the best thing we can do is make a wrong decision. Both will grow us and stretch us and teach us. You'll learn from life's on-ramps, inroads, and freeways as much as from life's U-turns, detours, and dead ends.

Asking my wife to marry me was one of the best decisions I've made, but she wasn't the first woman I dated. By spending time with women who were wrong for me, I was better prepared for the one who was best. Similarly, a few of the jobs I've had have failed. After leaving college, I worked on a U.S. Senate race in Alaska that ended in disaster. I interned at a sports radio station only to find out there wasn't a future for me there. I developed television segments in unsustainable formats that I was never able to sell. If life had a rewind button, would I go back and avoid what some might call "wrong" decisions? No. They were necessary for getting me to where I now stand, the career I'm currently in. Looking back, I'm grateful that I made those leaps rather than languished and lingered. I realize that the way I executed those decisions and the lessons they taught me were more valuable than the decisions themselves.

Most people develop the habit of indecision early on. We arrive at college, unsure of our life's path. We refuse to choose a major because we haven't chosen a career. We feel pressured to identify our dream job as freshmen, when what we need most is to take a step forward. Credit hours disappear into thin air with wasted tuition money until we finally make a selection.

After college, the prospect of committing ourselves to one company induces sweat and panic. As indecision sets in, we hang our diplomas on the wall and begin waiting tables. Years later, we calm down and settle into a nine-to-five. After a few years in our chosen field, we develop a nagging restlessness that we should make a career change. We reason with ourselves, explaining that the notion is crazy and will just confirm to our friends and family that we are the flakes they suspected we were. The threat of the unknown and the comfort of our current jobs cause our feet to drag.

Weeks, months, years go by. In our twilight years we finally "make it." We're the ones in charge, the ones pulling the strings. But our fingers freeze. Should we invest in a new building and hire new employees? Would it be better to sell the company or double down? The habit of indecision that began as a surface scratch in our youth has now bled into every stage of life.

Here's the point: if we don't sow the seeds of decisiveness early in life, we'll reap the bitter fruit of indecision until we draw our final breath. Select the restaurant, and feast with your friends. Choose the movie, and let it bring full-belly laughter into your life. Decide to find your true calling, and don't let the tough choices paralyze you. The choice to take a step in *any* direction will always move you forward.

nineteen: Distractions

Scott Belsky
New York Times Bestselling Author

Three innovators and three dates converged to create a perfect storm in my life. On February 4, 2004, Mark Zuckerberg launched Thefacebook from his Harvard University dormitory. I wouldn't discover Facebook until a few years later, but once I did, it became the ultimate distraction. At the end of a long workday, I'd find myself commenting to my wife, "I didn't get everything done that I needed to today. I just ran out of time." She would sometimes reply, "You found time to make new friends on Facebook." Her words were a slight jab, the kind that spouses are good at offering, but it pulled back the curtain on my new distraction.

On March 21, 2006, Jack Dorsey launched Twitter as a micro-blogging tool whereby users could share their thoughts in 140-character snippets. I wasn't an early adopter in that case, but once I joined the service, @kencoleman found himself unable to resist sharing his thoughts. I interviewed Jack Dorsey a few years later, and although part of me wanted to simply thank him for his innovative genius, another part wanted to tell him how much of a daily distraction Twitter could be.

On January 9, 2007, Steve Jobs released the first iPhone to the waiting world. He didn't know that it would one day become an iconic device with 45 percent market share in users. Or maybe he did; he was Steve Jobs, after all. I purchased the first model of iPhone, and something about it—maybe it was the ESPN apps or instant access to new sites—glued it to my hand. Once this device was fitted with Facebook and Twitter, I found myself swirling in the Bermuda Triangle of techno-logical distractions.

I grew increasingly absent mentally and emotionally. My kids would be holding up their latest school project and chanting, "Daddy, look" while I responded with a disconnected "Mmm-hmm" until the fourth or fifth iteration. I texted during dinner dates with my wife, stepped away from family time to check Twitter, and updated my Facebook status when I should have been working.

The breaking point came one night after a rare trip when I'd been away from my family for five days. I came bursting in the door just before dinner, and my children and wife greeted me with the sweet-est hugs and kisses. My wife was almost done cooking in the kitchen, so I took my kids into the adjoining living room for some premeal wrestling. A few minutes into our horseplay, I got a text and stepped away to respond. We wrestled for a moment more; then the text I'd sent gave me an idea for a tweet. I darted around the corner to type it. Just as I re-entered our homemade arena, the phone rang, and I took the call. There I was, holding my children at bay while I responded to the madness.

My wife quietly watched from the kitchen. When I got off the phone, she called my name with that tone that all husbands know means trouble. I entered the kitchen, and she calmly said, "Ken, your kids haven't seen their daddy in five days. But every time they try to spend time with you, you're too distracted by your phone calls and text messages. They need you to disconnect for a minute."

She was right. I don't want my kids' lasting impression of their fa-ther to be that while he was among them, he was always chin down and nose deep in his iPhone. I don't want them to remember me as a dad who valued tweets more than quality time with them.

That night flashed through my mind as I spoke with Scott Belsky a couple of years later. Scott is the founder and CEO of Behance, a company that produces goods and services for creative industries. He is also the bestselling author of *Making Ideas Happen: Overcoming the Ob-stacles Between Vision and Reality*. He is an expert on moving ideas from the lightbulb moment to reality, so I wanted to know what he thought about technology and its effect on our overall effectiveness.

KC: Technology has created an all-access culture in business, making us busier and more distracted from the effort required to make things happen. How do we protect our time and effort?

SB: I think it's important for us to recognize that we're entering this era of what I like to call a reactionary workflow. And what that means is that you can wake up and have more inbox emails, more Twitter messages and Facebook messages and LinkedIn messages, and the list goes on and on. You could spend all your day reacting to whatever's come in to you, living essentially someone else's to-do list rather than being proactive in focusing on what you are most passionate about.

This is a really scary time. If you live a life of reactionary workflow, then you're never going to make an impact on what matters most to you over time.

I would dare to say that the last sort of sacred space of deep thinking where we can actually think proactively about the long term is probably the shower. Is there any other space that hasn't already been penetrated with the constant inflow of information? And now, of course, they have shower media centers and you can have Twitter streaming in your shower, so we've almost lost that.

So we need to force ourselves to have thinking time rather than rely on circumstance to allow for thinking and focusing on priorities. And during those periods of time, we need to shut off all of these other

> "If you live a life of reactionary workflow, then you're never going to make an impact on what matters most to you over time."

distractions. We need to organize a list of two to three other things that we want to focus on in the long term, and we need to start sinking into it. I call them the "windows of nonstimulation" in our day. We all need them. During those periods of time, we need to think about the goals that we're really, really working toward. Otherwise, we are just going to be at the mercy of the last email.

Many great ideas have come into being as a result of technology. But after speaking to Scott, I wonder how many great ideas have failed to come into being *because of* technology. As he points out, technology has become a modern-day slave master. It chains us to our devices from which we fear running away as we fight off phantom vibrations. Emails can no longer wait; they must be answered within minutes. Phone calls are a must-take. And our thoughts and reflections on just about everything must be posted quickly before today's headlines become old news. Many modern Americans live in captivity, enslaved to the inbox, iPhone, and Internet.

Yet I suspect that if we read Belsky's words and respond by demonizing technology, setting aside our cell phones, or committing Facebook suicide, we'll have missed his larger point. Technology's tools are not inherently depraved, but they become so when they are improperly stewarded. Good things become bad things when they take us away from the most important things.

If asked about our greatest priorities, most of us would name our spouse, our children, our friends, or our occupational passions. Yet our lives tell a different story when those things are relegated to the back burner at the beckoning of others. What do you claim are your priorities? Does the rhythm of your day bear that out?

My wife's gentle but revealing words that evening made me realize that I needed to steward the distractions in my own life better. I was sacrificing the important on the altar of the immediate, and as a result, I was missing memories with my family. I'm working hard now to keep those disturbances from reigning over my life. When life's perfect storms rage, we can't avoid the rain. But we don't have to get stuck in the downpour.

twenty: Letting Go

Henry Cloud
Clinical Psychologist and *New York Times* Bestselling Author

In the 1990s, Jarrod was the CEO of a large tech company. Under his leadership, the organization thrived. Profits rose each year. Jarrod's commanding presence silenced any room he entered, but his kind eloquence quickly eased those he spoke with. I always expected Jarrod to end up on the cover of *Fortune* or *Fast Company*, assuming he'd retire early and join a speaking circuit. He was destined for corporate lunches and executive leadership seminars.

Then the phone rang.

Jarrod's voice was cracking on the other end of the line. He told me that his wife had caught him having an extramarital affair. As word spread of his malfeasance, many of his friends and employees had lost respect for him. His family and career were crumbling before his eyes.

During the months that followed, he lost credibility in his work. He lacked the confidence he'd once had to control conversations and close business deals. His company's profits fell, his employees' morale tanked, and the organization's board of trustees finally issued a vote of no confidence. Lacking the financial resources to sustain himself and his fracturing family, Jarrod filed for bankruptcy.

Time crept by, but Jarrod failed to get back on his feet. He tried to launch a new company, but he was only a shadow of the leader he'd been. The venture crumbled within months. His wife wouldn't forgive him, but she wouldn't divorce Jarrod either. Each day he walked back into a hostile home where he was forced to relive the mistakes he'd made. Bitterness grew in his heart.

Nearly twenty years have passed, and Jarrod still hasn't gotten back on the horse. His wife can't forgive him, and he hasn't forgiven himself either. He's a nomad, wandering aimlessly to rediscover his identity.

Maybe your story is like Jarrod's. You made a poor business decision that shipwrecked you, or you failed morally. You can't seem to glue the pieces of your life back together. You've paid for your sins, and you'd like to move on. How can you let go of your failures and move forward?

Dr. Henry Cloud is a psychologist, leadership consultant, and bestselling author whose books have sold more than six million copies, including the two-million-seller *Boundaries: When to Say YES, When to Say NO, to Take Control of Your Life*. With his combination of clinical and leadership experience, he seemed the perfect person to shed light on why some people recover from failures and others turn out like Jarrod.

KC: Advising a bitter friend to "just let it go" is easy, but moving past one's pain, anger, and failures can be challenging. How can we properly respond to setbacks and pursue a healthy and confident future?

HC: It actually has a lot to do with how the brain works and how character is constructed. Some people process failures and setbacks and losses well, and some people don't.

One thing that is common among those who don't deal well with these things is that they personalize the failure. They don't see it as just one event but instead as having meaning about them as a person, i.e., they are "not good enough." They also generalize from that one event to their whole life or their whole business or the whole industry or everything they do as being bad. And then they add a time dimension to it, thinking they will always be in this bad place, and it starts to cloud their view of the future. And when you see failures or setbacks this way, it makes a huge difference.

People who handle these situations well tend to not personalize it. If Tiger Woods hits a shot out of bounds, he doesn't think he's a crummy golfer. If Peyton Manning throws an interception, he doesn't think he is a loser. Instead, they wonder what went wrong with that shot or that play or what they need to adjust. They actually use failures as a feedback clue to coach them and train them as opposed to letting those events define who they are. In fact, the highest performers are not attached to results at all. One outcome doesn't define them. They treat it more objectively.

We often don't understand that our self-evaluations have been internalized from outside voices. What really strong performers do to overcome setbacks is more than just forgive themselves. They usually have some key relationships with their coaches, team members, mentors, buddy, or whoever helps them to let go of failures and setbacks. Therefore, they interpret failures differently because of these relationships. Because they are forgiven and accepted, they are encouraged to learn from failure and they find out it doesn't have to affect the future. They internalize that encouragement from the outside, and it becomes a part of their own thinking over time. This is why it's really important to create supportive learning teams around ourselves as opposed to firing squads.

One of the most important things is how you see your life's narrative. If the way you interpret any event is part of a bigger picture, a longer story that understands that life will have wins and losses, but that overall it is headed in a good direction, no one setback will do you in. Every movie has some scenes that are bad, but it turns around by the end. In a lifetime of business, markets go down, economies crash, you lose some customers, but that is just part of it. In a marriage, there will be some conflicts and tough moments, but the overall love story is a good one. You realize that negative chapters can still get you to a good ending in the larger narrative, so you keep living the story.

That does incredible things in the functioning of the brain. It will determine whether you go into fight-or-flight mode in a tough season or instead are able to engage judgment and higher reasoning capacities so you successfully work through the obstacles. Therefore, people's narrative really organizes the software of how they work through this stuff and achieve well after it's over.

People who personalize setbacks struggle to let go. Rather than seeing the setbacks as failures, they see *themselves* as failures. Those who stumble must learn to see downfalls as scars rather than open wounds. A scar reminds us of the injury, but an open wound continues to hurt us and often leads to infection. If we cannot move beyond our missteps, our failure begins to fester.

Cloud reminds us that we must see life as a narrative filled with both positive and negative chapters. Like every good story, life is filled with tension, struggle, and moments of frustration. The main character may experience devastation, but the tale continues to unfold. Seasoned readers know that even narratives filled with negative chapters can have happy endings. So it is with life.

No failure is so terminal, so fatal that we're forced onto the shelf of life. When we fail, we must seek forgiveness from everyone we've hurt. And we must forgive ourselves. We can't glue the pieces back together, but we don't have to live in the carnage either. As we release life's disappointments, we come to realize that one can experience failure without being defined by it.

twenty-one:
Difficult Relationships

Les Parrott
Cofounder of the Center for Relationship Development and
New York Times Bestselling Author

Unless you've been stranded on an island with a volleyball named Wilson, you have people in your life who make you want to drink bourbon out of a cereal bowl. When you are a teenager, your parents make that list. "No" seems to be their favorite word. Their rules seem more fit for an Alcatraz inmate than a churchgoing B student. Your mom seems to tap phone calls with your girlfriend on par with the CIA. Your dad lives vicariously through you, pressing you to achieve all the dreams he left behind.

Then you grow up, and you begin to respect them. Their ludicrous eccentricities now make all the sense in the world. You find yourself asking advice from the very ones you believed were helplessly detached from reality. But now Aunt Ethel fills that spot. Or Uncle Leroy. Or perhaps your overbearing sister-in-law slides in. They brag incessantly about their bratty hellions, while they attempt to lecture you on how to raise your own better. Rather than listen to your current woes, they attempt to fix all your problems. You haven't asked for their advice, but they don't seem to care.

Perhaps the tension originates from outside the family. Your boss seems to lack emotions common among his fellow *Homo sapiens*. He remains oblivious to every victory you achieve, but he never fails to notice your mistakes. The guy at work relishes giving you unsolicited advice, and each time he does, you consider resorting to violence. The negativity from your neighbors has driven you indoors, but they always seem to pressure you into going to more miserable dinner parties. One of the women who shares your spin class can't seem to resist flirting with your husband. Every fiber of your being wants to sit in your revving minivan and wait for her to cross the street.

Sometimes—dare I say many times—we are the difficult person. I'm a crusader by nature. I have to resist pitching a fit about poor service from a waitress or calling the manager of a retail store whose salesperson speaks curtly to customers. My friends and family would tell you that I can be difficult, driven to such a posture by other difficult people. I love to fix problems, but often my best efforts actually heighten the tension I'm seeking to eliminate. Regardless of the source of tension, the problem remains: we all struggle to deal with the annoying, frustrating, exasperating, difficult people in our lives.

Les Parrott specializes in dealing with people like this. He is a cofounder of the Center for Relationship Development at Seattle Pacific University, a program dedicated to teaching the basics of healthy relationships. He is also author of several bestselling books, including *Saving Your Marriage Before It Starts* and *Relationships: How to Make Bad Relationships Better and Good Relationships Great*. If anyone can illuminate the darkness when it comes to managing relationships, it's Les.

KC: Avoiding difficult people—whether in our family, our community, or at work—seems impossible. How can we manage the tension these relationships bring into our lives and interact with difficult people effectively?

LP: Three things come to my mind when I think about how to cope with difficult people. They come from the research for a book I wrote called *High-Maintenance Relationships*. One of the things I discovered is that everybody is somebody's high-maintenance relationship some of the time. And yet there are certain people who just seem to make our lives more difficult than they need to be on a regular basis. I have learned that there are at least three ways to make life easier and cope more effectively with these folks.

One, it is very helpful to see the dark side of yourself that is reflected in that person. In other words, you have to tune in to how you are just like the person who is driving you nuts. More often than not, the person who really makes our life difficult is pushing a button that reminds us of somebody we do not want to be. So if we can own that part of ourselves, we will end up having more control over it within ourselves and are less likely to be annoyed by it.

That leads to a second thing, which is summed up by a single word: objectivity. A healthy person has the capacity to stand back from a difficult relationship with an attitude that basically says, "Well, this should be interesting." The person becomes more of an observer and does not get sucked into the emotion of the interaction with the difficult person. This allows you to not get worn down and bent out of shape and feeling frustrated, because you are just observing "Isn't it interesting the way this person seems to go about his life?"

The third thing is probably the most important. In fact, I often tell people if there is one thing I can do to help you in your relationship, I would press the magic button to give you an abundance of this quality. It is empathy: the capacity to put yourself in someone else's shoes and see the world as he or she sees it.

That sounds really simple, and most people, when they think about it, say, "Yeah, I do that. I am really good at that." But we know from research that the vast majority of us may think we are good at it, but we really are not. Empathy requires both your head and your heart. It requires sympathizing as well as analyzing. It is like two wings of an airplane. If you really want to empathize, you have to use both your head and your heart, and that is why it is a challenge.

Most of us are pretty good at one or the other but not both. We may be really good at sympathizing and feeling somebody else's feelings. Or we're good at analyzing, at backing up and saying "Well, this is what this person needs to be doing." But to have a combination of both of skills is a real challenge. So you must learn to put yourself in somebody else's shoes. It will give you far more grace, far more compassion, far more understanding. And it will fuel a sense of objectivity and a sense of self-reflection.

When you focus on these three things, you will soon be amazed at how easy those difficult relationships become.

Les points out that the characteristics or habits we dislike in others are often the ones we loathe in ourselves. Oftentimes we find ourselves gossiping about a gossip or criticizing someone for being negative, failing to realize that we are guilty of the very same sin. Perhaps we grow more aware of the flaws we see each morning in the mirror, similar to the way we begin to notice particular automobiles on the road after we purchase one ourselves. As Hermann Hesse once said, "If you hate a person, you hate something in him that is part of yourself."

"More often than not, the person who really makes our life difficult is pushing a button that reminds us of somebody we do not want to be."

Realizing that we share the flaws we despise is helpful. Such discipline replaces antipathy with empathy. When we begin to see that we share those problems, grace and humility grow within us. This posture can even catapult us to work on ourselves.

By nurturing empathy for the difficult people in our lives—by learning to put ourselves into somebody else's shoes, as Parrott states it—we alleviate much tension. The hypocritical human tendency desires grace on our bad days but fails to recognize when others need the same. Often a waitress's rudeness can be attributed to a dead-end job, a rebellious child, or a cheating husband. A retail salesperson may have a bad attitude, but he may be going through a nasty divorce. Crossing their paths, we assume we're the target, but in reality, we just stepped unwittingly into the cross fire.

Parrott calls for grace, compassion, and understanding. I can't help believing that the pain of difficult relationships would be less if we focused on nurturing such characteristics. What if the next time your boss or annoying family member makes a snarky comment, you smile and walk away? Or, better yet, you redouble your effort to win that person over? The discomfort of that relationship might lighten, and your response might serve as a reminder that difficulties don't have to make one difficult.

twenty-two: Forgiveness

Gayle Haggard
New York Times Bestselling Author and Wife of
Fallen Pastor Ted Haggard

After seven years of failed efforts to get pregnant, Stacy and I stepped back to regroup. We'd exhausted our patience with natural methods, and fertility tests provided no explanation. In Vitro hadn't worked; our doctors were confounded because they considered us perfect candidates. The only pregnancy option left was egg donation or a surrogacy, but we had both been feeling our hearts open to adoption.

Once we made the decision, we ran a gauntlet of background checks, a home study, and an excruciating period of waiting to see if any prospective birth mothers would select our profile. Then one day our phone rang. An unknown area code flashed across the caller ID screen. An adoption adviser from the Midwest informed me that we'd been selected by a birth mother and needed to fly out to meet her immediately. She was already in labor with what could become our baby boy.

My wife and I entered frantic mode, rushing to Walmart to purchase as many baby necessities as we could think of, all the while calling airlines to check available flights. Stacy booked our tickets while I packed the car. Before we had time to completely process the ordeal, we were in the air.

We landed and headed to the hospital. The concoctions in our stomachs were equal parts shock, anxiety, and excitement. After what seemed like hours, we arrived at the maternity ward.

Though the child had been born, we were taken to meet the birth mother first. I can't explain how surreal it is to stand before someone who has chosen you to parent the child she gave birth to. Humility filled my heart. And nervousness.

Her face was sweet, but her eyes carried the weight of the pain she'd just been through. Stacy and I stumbled over our words as we expressed our mutual gratitude. The woman returned thanks. She said she was glad her son was going to be placed into a loving home like ours. Poverty had followed her for many years, she explained, and she simply couldn't afford the burden of raising this child. Our hearts broke when she stared out the window and explained that she'd never even seen the ocean.

"Are you ready to meet the little guy?" our adviser asked.

We nodded.

Before we entered the NICU, she explained that the child had been born prematurely. We should not be shocked if he appeared smaller than normal. At that she opened the door, and we crept toward the crib. A warming lamp hung over his head, and the small pink-skinned body squirmed in a fresh diaper. Stacy and I froze in awe, knowing that the process of falling in love with the boy had already begun. Serenity filled the room as we scooped up his tiny body and held him close to our chests. Over the next few hours, we cried tears of joy over him, sang and cooed to him, and covered his bald head in kisses. We had no idea that that would be the last moment of peace we'd experience for some time.

After we exited the infant room, the doctors pulled us aside to tell us they had found amphetamines in the baby's system.

"It's not from Sudafed," one remarked, implying that they believed that his mother had used illegal drugs during pregnancy. "He seems fine now, but you never know what could happen in the days or even years ahead."

We headed back to meet with the birth mother, trying to get to the bottom of whatever was happening. "We have been told that the baby has amphetamines in his system and two possible birth fathers have come forward," I said, my voice cracking. "We need to know the truth." Tears began pouring down my face, and I stooped down to one knee. Stacy sobbed uncontrollably. "I'm begging you to tell us the truth. Please. I'm begging you," I said.

Before she opened her mouth, I knew I she was about to bathe us in lies. She told us that she had never taken drugs and she had been honest about her sexual history. Her cold face destroyed my resolve, and we left. As the day unfolded, test results showed that the boy's mother had been using illegal drugs.

As if that were not difficult enough to process, a nurse later informed us that two additional men had stepped forward, both claiming to be the birth father. Both planned to contest the adoption. That had forced the state to take custody of the child. We were no longer allowed to see the child and were advised to return home. We didn't weep on the journey back. There were no tears left to cry. Our tear ducts were as numb as our hearts. Blank stares and clamped jaws defined our faces as Stacy and I stood with hands clasped.

The next day, we flew home, exhausted and disappointed. As I lay in bed that evening, anguish turned to anger. How could the birth mother do this to us? Why would she lie to us? And God, how could you let us walk down this road only to break our hearts again? My inaudible questions received no answer and festered in the night's shadows.

Over the next six weeks, the adoption agency's lawyer called each day to give us updates, and with every call, I grew more bitter. Then one day, I was reading a book of Bible promises on faith and trust, and my heart softened. Each word of Scripture was like a meat tenderizer on my hardened heart. I phoned the agency's attorney. "What would you do if you were me?" I asked.

He paused, then replied, "You need to let it go."

At those words, Stacy and I decided to forgive and move on.

The images from that ordeal flashed through my mind like a slide show as I waited to interview Gayle Haggard. She is the wife of Ted Haggard, a former megachurch pastor and president of the National Association of Evangelicals. In the fall of 2006, Ted was accused of having a sexual affair with another man while taking illegal drugs. He later admitted to those moral failures and resigned from all leadership positions. Gayle felt humiliated and betrayed by the man she loved. But whereas most women would have run from their marriage's mess and media flurry, she decided to forgive her husband and stay with him.

"His world was getting so dark, and I decided 'I am going in after him,'" she later said. "'I'm not going to let this destroy his life if I can help it.'"[1]

Unlike the "good wife" caricature displayed on television and in film, Gayle is a no-nonsense woman with a heart of compassion. She walked with Ted through a process of counseling and healing—a journey told in her bestselling book, *Why I Stayed: The Choices I Made in My Darkest Hour*. I wanted to know what she could share about learning to forgive when we've been deeply wounded.

KC: What do we have to do to truly begin the process of forgiving, and how does forgiveness work itself out?

GH: I think forgiveness is easy to talk about and a lot harder to do. Once we determine that we are going to forgive, we set our trajectory toward forgiveness, but oftentimes it involves a process we must work through. In my life, what I had to work out was that I had chosen to forgive Ted, but then I had to deal with the reality of our situation. I was suffering tremendous pain and loss along with a host of other people I cared about, including our children and our church. Even though I faced my painful emotions and chose to relinquish them and to forgive, I found they kept circling around again. Something would trigger them, and I would once again feel the anger and the sense of betrayal and loss. I would have to choose again to forgive Ted.

Something that helped me in this process was understanding that Ted was hurting too. He felt responsible, yet he carried the weight of embarrassment, shame, and failure. One of the most important components of my forgiveness process was working to understand his pain and how he got into the situation he was in. The more knowledge I gained, the more I was able to sort out what needed to be forgiven and what just needed to be understood. Ted took responsibility for the choices he made and the pain he caused. I, however, took responsibility for trying to understand and to have compassion for him. I wanted to see him the way God sees him.

All of this is involved in the forgiveness process—gaining understanding, growing in empathy and compassion, discovering what needs to be forgiven, and then really forgiving. I cannot tell you how often I would hear people say, "Oh, we forgive him." However, there was nothing in their actions that showed that they had forgiven him, and I think forgiveness needs to mean something. I think we need to forgive the way God forgives. Ultimately, when the process is done, it is as though the person never sinned.

Certainly, there may be natural consequences that will take their course. We may also have to deal with emotions that reemerge, but we have to release the person from that sense that we want to punish him, that he owes us, or that we want to hold over him what he has done wrong. As long as we feel that way toward the person, no one receives any benefits from our claim of forgiveness—not us, not him.

While working through my process, I repeatedly had imaginations emerge in my mind, as you might imagine when there has been betrayal or unfaithfulness. I had to deal with those thoughts. I finally settled the fact that I could not keep doing this to him. We had been through this, and we were no better for continually bringing it up again. I told him that I forgave him. I decided not to scrutinize him anymore. I chose to let my love for him cover his sins.

> "The more knowledge I gained, the more I was able to sort out what needed to be forgiven and what just needed to be understood."

Once I finally settled that, I felt my heart begin to heal, and we began to move forward. Whenever imaginations or accusing thoughts would try to reemerge, I reminded myself of my decision to let my love for him cover over those things. As time went on, those thoughts progressively diminished. I really believe that that is the kind of genuine forgiveness God extends to all of us. When he forgives us, he really does forgive us.

I've discovered that forgiveness strengthens the bonds of our relationships in surprising ways and often we are better off than we were before. I know that has proven true in my life. Ted's and my marriage is more solid, more understanding, and more intimate. And we are happier together in our marriage than we have ever been.

We often say, "Forgive and forget," but it's really not possible. You can't wipe out hurts from your memory. Visual or verbal triggers may cause you to relive the situation. You can't forget that your loved one has cheated on you or that your business partner stole from you. But you *can* refuse to obsess over it and let it determine how you treat others. The scar can remain without festering.

As Gayle reminds us, forgiveness isn't an act as much as a process. It may require sitting down to dinner with someone you despise or taking the first step in restoring a relationship in which trust has been violated. Forgiveness may mean praying a blessing over the one who hurt you. It may mean saying "Even though I've been deeply wounded, I'm *choosing* not to dwell there. I'm *choosing* not to hold it against you." Those acts will rarely happen only once. The offended will have to repeat the choice to forgive again and again until the process of forgiveness is complete. Like love, it involves a commitment with subsequent moments of recommitment.

I'd like to say that once Stacy and I determined we would forgive, we never thought about the ordeal again. But I'd be lying. Though I did feel more peaceful about moving forward, the anger and hurt didn't go away. We had simply begun walking the path of forgiveness. Looking back, Stacy and I feel the way Gayle does: we don't know why God allowed the experience to happen, but we're stronger for having come through it together.

twenty-three: Redemption

Jack Abramoff
America's Most Notorious Lobbyist

With our three children in tow, Stacy and I rushed along the bustling city sidewalks. In an effort not to be late for lunch, people became obstacles that must be dodged rather than followed. We'd dart left, then right, glancing over our shoulders to confirm that we hadn't lost a child in the maneuver. Every few feet, the crowds would clear and my eyes would lift above the chaos to the skyscrapers above. The glass-and-steel sentinels of downtown Atlanta have always fascinated me.

That morning, our family was meeting some close friends for breakfast at the Westin Peachtree Plaza. The cylindrical icon stretches seventy-three stories overhead and is the second tallest hotel in the Western Hemisphere. The uppermost levels house the Sun Dial, a three-floor revolving restaurant boasting the best aerial views of Atlanta and accessible only by an exhilarating eighty-five-second ride in an exterior glass elevator.

My kids had never visited the Sun Dial before, so I watched their expressions as the elevator rocketed upward. 36 . . . 41 . . . 53 . . . their eyes widened with each passing floor. The ding signaled our arrival, and the doors parted at the seam. My children froze as they stared at the expanse beyond the windows in front of us. No one spoke a word as we gazed out on our city for miles, even beyond the urban edge.

Conversation is difficult when one dines at the Sun Dial. The rotating restaurant provides patrons with ever-changing scenery. To the south, I looked out upon one of the busiest airports in the world, and to the north, I peered at the busy midtown streets. When facing west,

I could see CNN's world headquarters. Toward the east, I could make out the frame of Stone Mountain, the largest exposed hunk of granite in the world. I tried to engage in the breakfast dialogue, but all I could think about was that this thriving metropolis had once lain in ruin.

Had I stood in the same location where the Westin now stands a century and a half ago, I'd have been ankle deep in ashes. In September 1864, Union General William T. Sherman besieged Atlanta. When the Confederate Army finally retreated, Sherman sent a letter to Atlanta's mayor, telling him that he would, without a doubt, burn his city to the ground. He wrote, "Now you must go, and take with you the old and feeble, feed and nurse them, and build for them, in more quiet places, proper habitations to shield them against the weather until the mad passions of men cool down, and allow the Union and peace once more to settle over your old homes in Atlanta."[1] The military leader who made famous the phrase "War is hell" proved his maxim was true as he razed the southern city.

But Atlantans' spirit was not destroyed forever. They returned to their city and rebuilt it brick by brick and stone by stone. Today, the seal of Atlanta is engraved with a phoenix, the mythical bird that burns itself only to be reborn from the flames. The creature rises from flames on our city's seal underneath the word *resurgens*. The Latin term means "rising again."

More than history, Atlanta's story is a metaphor for life. You don't have to live very long to realize that the world is filled with fires. Bankruptcy, divorce, miscarriages, cancer, depression—these maladies are only a few of the flames that can incinerate our lives. They leave us gasping for air, weeping in the shower, and staring blankly into darkness as we beg ourselves to fall asleep. When those fires inevitably rage, one must wrestle with a profound question: will I ever rise again?

Jack Abramoff is known as "America's most notorious lobbyist." An extensive investigation in 2006 uncovered the gross corruption of political lobbying. Abramoff routinely offered luxurious trips, expensive dinners, and concert tickets to high-ranking politicians in exchange for various political kickbacks. He maintained four skyboxes at major sporting arenas at a cost of more than a million dollars per year that he would use to influence public policy.[2]

His face was plastered on newspapers and televisions around the country, and his scandalous story became the basis of the feature film *Casino Jack*, in which Kevin Spacey played Abramoff. The investigation led to the conviction of two White House officials, nine lobbyists and congressional aides, and Representative Bob Ney, but Abramoff became the poster child for Washington corruption. I wanted to know what he, just released from federal prison, had learned about rising again.

KC: You are attempting to lead a productive life, to add value to society. But as you consider the past few years—your indictment, your conviction, your incarceration—what have you learned about grace, restoration, and redemption?

JA: I am still learning, obviously, because my process and journey continues to develop, and mine is still at its nascent stages. But having said that, I've come through a maelstrom and a series of crucibles. I have learned that human beings can always be restored. There may be some things that we can never repair on Earth, but regardless of what we did or to where we sank, there is always the possibility that tomorrow will be better.

Only if we give up that hope, if we give up that belief, only then will things never be better. We must live with the belief that we can renew, we can remake, we can reinvent, and we can restore. Even if it is merely a belief and not reality, because belief itself is of value. Belief leads us to want to be better, to want to do good. I believed these concepts the way most people probably do deep down all their lives, but they became real for me when I had to actually live them—and I am still living them.

Even in the depths of despair of my situation, I always believed that there would be a tomorrow. There would be an opportunity for things to look brighter. It happens to be the case in my life that things are brighter today than they were while I was in prison, than when this calamity first came upon me. My moment of transformation came through moving from depression to a realization that life will not always be a fall into the abyss for me. I recognized that this will end. And that when it ends—even if it is merely my body lying crushed on the floor—it is better than the fall. The fall is the most dangerous part. Not where you wind up.

When I held on to hope, I knew that I may never get back to where I was but I could be grateful for where I am. The next day can only be better than where today is, so I can just take it one day at a time.

We can't escape reality. We're flawed and broken and mess up a lot. We need to be honest about who we are and what we do wrong. But we don't have to languish in it. There has to be honest recognition that our actions got us into this mess. No one forced Abramoff to commit his crimes. He is responsible. We can move from punishment to progress, from ruin to restoration. Most people never take responsibility for what has happened to them. We must accept responsibility if we want to move forward.

Tomorrow will be better. When you hit rock bottom, you have a choice to either accept where you are or you can change your position. You fell from a particular place and you may never get back there again, but you don't have to stay where you are either. Up is possible because there is no down when you sit at the bottom.

Jack Abramoff remains stained and stigmatized by his sins. But he recognizes that he doesn't have to dwell there. If you're still breathing and moving, restoration is possible. The only point at which redemption cannot be achieved is when we cease to exist.

If you're still breathing and moving, restoration is possible.

When we spoke, the upbeat tone in Jack's voice surprised me. He seemed truly grateful for where he sat, and there is wisdom in such a posture. The lower one falls, the greater the opportunity for growth and the more noticeable the progress. No one notices when a valedictorian gets an A on a test, but people will notice when a child on academic probation does. Comebacks are great only when the chasm crossed is great. The fallen can be grateful because they've been given a great opportunity.

Jack Abramoff is trying to capitalize on the opportunity in his life by attempting to right some of his wrongs. He has briefed FBI agents on the nature of K Street corruption, and he has penned a series of proposals for closing the revolving door between politicians and lobbyists. "What I want to do is something to undo what I did," he said in a recent television interview. "The hope is I can use my natural infamy in a positive way."[3]

Life is full of fires, but stories like Jack's give hope. When flames decimate your life and burn your skyscrapers to the ground, you can rebuild. Redemption is possible. *Resurgens.* You can rise again.

twenty-four: Starting Over

Dave Ramsey
Nationally Syndicated Radio Host and *New York Times*
Bestselling Author

As the workday ground to a stop, I began to doze. My eyelids had squeezed out the sunlight and my chin was beginning to fall when my phone rang and jolted me awake. An old friend from college, Danny, was calling to catch up and reminisce. We traded stories long forgotten and laughed. But suddenly the conversation fell solemn.

"Ken," Danny said, his voice trembling, "I called to give you some bad news."

A family friend had approached Danny's father some months earlier with a business opportunity. A wealthy retired man with millions in liquid capital, Danny's dad had decided to entrust a large sum of cash into his friend's care. Time had passed without much return on investment, and one day the FBI had showed up to inform Danny's parents that their money had been invested in a Ponzi scheme. All their invested capital had been lost, and their trusted friend now sat in a prison cell.

Despair reigned as the couple received the discouraging news. Danny's parents had invested their retirement cushion, and it was all lost. They'd gambled away their children's inheritance, and the shame was almost too much to bear. Tears fell from hopelessness and hurt, betrayal and bewilderment. What would the elderly couple do to recover from their losses? How would they survive without their life's savings?

Danny told me that his parents had come out of retirement and were looking for employment. They'd sold their cars and all possessions of significant value in order to pay their bills and avoid home foreclosure. My heart sank as I imagined the pain his family must be experiencing. I'd met his parents on several occasions. They were affable and hospitable, known for their generosity to local charities. Their calamity seemed unjust.

"I'm hurting for my mom and dad. They are out looking for jobs and scrounging to keep their bills paid," Danny said. "They are forced to start over."

Danny's family's story is all too common in the United States today—not the experience of embezzlement but the experience of profound loss. Home foreclosures have reached an all-time high, millions of people remain out of work, the age of retirement continues to climb, and consumer confidence remains low. Many people who find themselves ill equipped for the digital world are going back to school and changing careers late in life. As Americans face these realities, they're confronting the reality of starting over.

The nationally syndicated radio host Dave Ramsey can empathize with such misfortune. He was a successful real estate investor in Tennessee until one of his largest creditors was sold. The new bank demanded that he pay his notes and forced him into bankruptcy. Ramsey relaunched his career as a financial counselor, sharing the lessons he learned during his time of tragedy.

Today, he is one of the United States' most respected voices on financial stewardship. His nationally syndicated radio program, *The Dave Ramsey Show*, has spawned bestselling books and even a television show on the Fox Business Network from 2007 to 2010. When I spoke with Ramsey recently, I picked his brain on how people can successfully start over after failure.

KC: Encountering failure along the path to our dreams can be devastating. How do people recover when they fail and have to start again?

DR: Everyone who does anything of scale has a splat. The splat forms some of who you are for the rest of your life. The splat does not have to be fatal in business or marriage or your spiritual walk, but it hits you hard enough that you find yourself flat on your back.

Whether it was a complete business failure like I had, with a bankruptcy and a marriage hanging on by a thread, a moral failure, or getting fired from your dream job, whenever you find yourself in the valley, how do you sit back up and move on from there? You are scared, and you can't breathe. How do you recover from that? It is a great question that we must answer.

First, you have to recognize that when you're flat on your back, there's nowhere to look but up. That's the position, I think, God puts you in with a splat. So you get up because you don't have any other choice. You start moving because you have to pay the light bill, or you just have to put one foot in front of the other to function. You are grieving. You're reeling emotionally. You are a zombie, and you are just walking. But you put one foot in front of the other because literally you must buy groceries the next week and you need to figure out how. The ones who just lie there will die of hunger pretty soon. In that sense, the first motivator is not positive at all. You move out of desperation.

The next thing is that the fog in your head begins to clear. You just had your bell rung, but now you're beginning to see clearly again. You think past the moment. You start to get a little bit philosophical and theological, and you reassess the things that are real in your life. As we move forward, we recognize our values and principles, and from that point forward, they are seared into our souls and never change. This step is important because principles are what make great men and great women. They make great careers. They build empires. A solid, immovable foundation becomes your touchstone for everything you are going to do as you move forward.

After I failed, I recognized that I had to place God first. Now all decisions filter through that value. All fears are translated through that paradigm and priority. After God, it is Sharon and then the kids and then work. There has never been a confusion about what I value since I set those as my foundation. I think that is why I have been able to work so hard, be so busy, and still have a great marriage and great kids. Everyone who comes into my life knows I have three rules: Do not get between me and my God. Do not get between me and my wife. Do not get between me and my kids. These priorities are the results of my splat. They are the benefit. Failure sears those kinds of principles into your life.

Finally, once you've reestablished your core values, you have to start dreaming again. You must start to see a vision for the future. The good news is that your vision will be better than it was before because you're wiser now, having failed. My former pastor used to say that a man with experience is not at the mercy of a man with an opinion. After we fail, we no longer run on theory. You no longer run on academic insight. You run on non-negotiable principles that you put in place as a result of your splat experience.

Once you get past zombie land and the clouds start to clear and you're able to reestablish your nonnegotiables, then you start to dream again, and you'll find that the things that you thought were going to kill you did not. All the manure in the valley is now helping things grow in your life. And that's when you realize that you wouldn't be where you are without having experienced the splat.

We often see starting over as a negative thing. It's drudgery. It's our worst nightmare. But Ramsey reframes "splats" as an opportunity to reassess our priorities. Life moves at breakneck speed, and along the way we often lose sight of the values we once held dear. Success and stress blur the lines between the important and the immediate. Starting over allows us to rediscover the priorities that we once kept close: friends, family, faith.

> **Starting over allows us to rediscover the priorities that we once kept close: friends, family, faith.**

The benefit of this reboot is that we're better prepared to prioritize than we once were. When you're twenty-two and ambitious, you make choices based on what feels right or what someone else told you works. But when you fail at forty-two or fifty-two, you base your decisions on what you know is right and what you know works. Your successes and failures in the laboratory of life have left you with experience rather than mere theory.

I wouldn't wish Danny's parents' circumstances on anyone, but it dulls the pain when we embrace starting over as an opportunity rather than an obstacle, as a gift rather than a curse. By starting over, we get to live life the way we should have when we started out.

Life's storms are inevitable, but, as Ramsey reminds us, the clouds *will* clear. And when they do, the sun will illuminate your world once more.

SUSTAINING

twenty-five: Mastery

Daniel Pink
New York Times Bestselling Author

Stacy and I should have recognized the warning signs when we brought home the new dresser. Because the furniture was for our son Chase, we decided to purchase a cute but inexpensive item from a large warehouse store not far from our house. In retrospect, red flags were waving throughout the ordeal.

The dresser cost less than a nice dinner out with my wife, leaving that old adage that you get what you pay for cooing in my ear. The item came in a box that would fit nicely under a Christmas tree, and when we opened it up, no fewer than three hundred pieces of mass-produced parts tumbled onto our floor. Standing over the pile of screws, slats, and knobs, I cast a worried gaze at Stacy. After I'd assembled the flimsy furnishing, we pushed it against Chase's wall and began to fill it with his clothes. The fiberboard bowed and strained under the weight of folded children's apparel.

In the weeks that followed, knobs wobbled and drawers continued to droop. At the urging of my wife, I decided the dresser needed a tune-up. Though I'm mechanically challenged, I summoned the spirit of Bob Vila and attempted to restore the mass-produced nightmare. Hours later, I found myself ankle-deep in tools, duct tape, and frustration. With a deep sigh, I looked at Stacy and commented that I would give anything for a great piece of antique furniture.

Money was tight while I was growing up, forcing my parents to be creative and resourceful when buying furniture. When a need presented itself, Mom and Dad would put us in the car and we'd head down to an antiques store. The experience was like treasure hunting, except that we were looking for maple or oak instead of gold and rubies. Eventually my parents would spy the piece they wanted. It was often the most visually undesirable item in the store, ensuring a better price. We'd drag the relics into our house, musty and smelling of mildew. That's when the transformation began. My parents would clean the items, stain them, and set them in permanent resting places.

I remember the day my parents brought home the saddest-looking rocking chair. A dilapidated cane seat accented the soot-covered frame. Taking one look, I shook my head, thinking that *this* item was just too far gone. New life was impossible. For weeks, my parents stripped the wood down, replaced the seat, and restained it. The day they brought the final product into the living room, my jaw rested upon the floor. The chair was beautiful and became my favorite place to sit. To this day, the rocker remains in their living room.

Why has it survived so long? Because it was made by a master craftsman. Unlike the dresser that was suffering in Chase's room, antique furnishings were made by human hands with attention to quality and detail. A chasm of difference separates those items from the factory-produced goods you find in most stores today. The former was made by a master; the latter was produced by a machine.

Modern society seems to favor mass production, not just in furniture but from its citizens. We dress alike, behave similarly, and speak with a common vernacular. Thanks to the gifts of the digital age, anyone today can become an "expert." Such a situation leaves me wondering where the master craftsmen are today. Where are the unusual, custom-built leaders who seek to rise above the fray rather than run with the pack?

I decided to ask *New York Times* bestselling author Daniel Pink that very question. A former speechwriter to then Vice President Al Gore, he has studied social trends and the science of success in the twenty-first century. His books include *Drive: The Surprising Truth About What Motivates Us* and *A Whole New Mind: Why Right-Brainers Will Rule the Future*. If anyone could answer my question on mastery, I figured Daniel Pink could.

KC: In today's 24/7 media culture, "experts" are a dime a dozen. In contrast, a true master craftsman remains rare and valuable. How do we master our strengths to maximize our impact?

DP: It's a mix of factors. First, one of the most important things in achieving mastery is to recognize how you think about it in the first place. That is, when you look at your own capabilities, do you see them as fixed, unchangeable, and simply part of your DNA, like eye color? Or do you look at them as actually malleable, things you can improve, you can get better at?

Too many of us take that first view—that being good at something depends on whether you have it or you don't. The problem with that belief, as Carol Dweck and others have taught us, is that's incorrect. It's not how mastery works. Indeed, if you start with that belief—that you're either good at something or you're not—you won't achieve mastery. Period. But if you think you are capable of getting better at something, then you have a shot.

Second, along with thinking about mastery in the right way, the next component is what you actually do—because true mastery is really, really hard. I think that's one reason why few people achieve it. It requires enormous amounts of work and persistence. It requires time. It requires grit. It requires effort. It requires setbacks.

And many of us aren't willing to accept that deal. We want to achieve mastery without pain. And that's not possible.

Third, you also have to wrap your mind around this unhappy fact: you can never actually achieve mastery. You may remember the word "asymptote" from algebra. Imagine a curved line that can come close to reach a horizontal line but never actually touches it. That untouchable horizontal line is the asymptote. You can get closer and closer and closer to it, but you can never reach it. That's the nature of mastery.

I do not care how good you are at something, how blessed you are with the opportunity to improve, no one can ever achieve full mastery. Picasso never achieved full mastery. Marian Anderson never achieved full mastery. Kobe Bryant has never achieved full mastery. Mastery is an asymptote, and that makes it simultaneously frustrating and alluring.

So I think the way we can get better at achieving mastery is just to get real about what it takes. And what it takes is thinking about your ability as something you can change. It requires a lot of pain, effort, and hard work, and it brings a certain amount of frustration in realizing that you can never actually achieve it fully.

Pink's words transcend insight and enter the realm of encouragement. He reminds us that gifts are malleable and fluid. Yes, we're all born with certain gifts. But those gifts can grow, mature, and develop. Great men and women in any field recognize their natural gifts but then hone those gifts over time. If we believe that our level of mastery is only a function of our innate makeup, we will never reach our fullest potential. Professional athletes were born with great talent, but without developing that talent, they would have remained average amateurs.

> **If we believe that our level of mastery is only a function of our innate makeup, we will never reach our fullest potential.**

You can always get better. A master carpenter or professional baseball player will always tell you that no matter one's level of success, he can always build a better product or play a better game. If you could resurrect Leonardo da Vinci or Vincent van Gogh and ask him what his perfect work of art was, I doubt he would be able to name a single painting or sculpture. Perfection is impossible.

We must also accept that the process of development is painstaking. Thanks to films, we often get the impression that a great businessman or soldier or artist becomes who he is in an hour and a half rather than through months and years of practice. Larry Bird spent hours shooting three-pointers before and after practice. Tiger Woods hit thousands of golf balls as he refined his swing. Because humans' default mode is complacency, many fail to commit to developing their natural gifts.

They fail to achieve mastery not because they aren't talented, but because they aren't disciplined.

You have within you a few strengths that, if honed, will empower you to impact your world. The potential exists. You need only to locate those gifts, work hard at developing them, and never stop pushing higher and farther. Even if others recognize that you are very good at what you do, never forget that you can always get better. The things that spring from your hands will not be perfect, but, like the works of master craftsmen, they'll stand the test of time.

twenty-six: Accountability

Tony Dungy
Former Championship Coach of the Indianapolis Colts and
New York Times Bestselling Author

"Have you heard the news?" a friend of mine asked frantically.

"What news?"

"About the Penn State scandal," he replied.

I ripped open my computer and quickly directed the browser to ESPN, where I discovered tragedy in more detail than I was prepared to handle. From 1994 until 2009, former Penn State University assistant football coach Jerry Sandusky had allegedly had inappropriate contact or sexually assaulted at least eight underage boys on or around university property. High-level school officials had been notified throughout those years, but they had failed to take aggressive action to prevent repeated occurrences. As a result, university president Graham Spanier was forced to resign and the iconic football head coach Joe Paterno was fired midseason.

The words on my screen burned that crisp November day of 2011 into my memory, and I was filled with anger. As a parent, I was outraged that those children's lives had been ruined because of the desire to protect the Penn State brand. If that had been one of my sons, I would have been filled with anger, confusion, hurt, and betrayal. Other than the death of one's child, a situation like this must be one of parents' greatest fears. I cannot accurately predict what my response would have been. Perhaps the accused would be awaiting autopsy rather than trial. Sadly, the people who had been most at fault had not been directly

131

involved in the situation, but they had allegedly allowed it to go on to protect the reputation of the university and its football program.

Stories like these are far too common in the sports world. I had been mystified when a scandal broke earlier in the same year about Jim Tressel, who was on his way to becoming a coaching deity at Ohio State. Tressel's players had been illegally selling memorabilia, and though he testified to the NCAA that he had had no prior knowledge of the impropriety, he later admitted that he had been well aware of it. He was forced to resign for both the actions of his players and his attempts to cover them up.

Both cases involve seemingly good men who developed a warped perspective that often creeps in with the acquisition of great influence. Careers that often begin with the highest integrity are clouded by a sense of self-protection, brand protection, or institutional protection. The mind-set stretches into the arenas of politics and business and even religion. One has only to look to the Catholic abuse scandals or the corporate corruption of the 1990s to see the storyline rippling out. But it seems to be endemic to sports as well.

When I think of great leaders in the sports world who were able to maintain their integrity, however, the name Tony Dungy comes to mind. Coach Dungy served as head coach of the Tampa Bay Buccaneers from 1996 to 2001 and the Indianapolis Colts from 2002 to 2008. In Indianapolis, he became the first African-American NFL coach to win a Super Bowl, forever enshrining him in the halls of football greatness. Dungy is known by his former players and colleagues for being a person of unwavering character and commitment to principle, so I wanted to hear how he had been able to achieve success while maintaining his integrity.

KC: It seems that no matter what channel of life we're working in, the more success we achieve, the greater temptation we face to compromise our integrity. You've had great success and also maintained your character. How can we maintain our integrity despite our level of influence, power, and success?

TD: I think we can get caught up in chasing success. We can get caught up in chasing financial gain or promotion, and the world says you do those things at all costs because they are the most important things. But to stay grounded, you really have to understand God's principles and what the Bible says about all that. Number one, serving the Lord is the most important thing, and second is building relationships with people. If you keep that in mind, it helps you stay grounded and not give in to the temptation to chase those other things. Nothing's wrong with financial gain and business success, but you can't pursue them at all costs.

I think accountability is really important, especially the higher up you go. I found that as you climb the ladder and you go from, say, assistant coach to a defensive coordinator to head coach to maybe president and general manager of a team, you have fewer and fewer people who are going to say, "Hey, boss, this is not exactly right" or "This is something you need to be concerned about." The higher up you go, the less of those people you'll find. So you've got to keep that accountability in your life, whether it's your spouse, your pastor, or good friends who have known you forever. Stay in a place of accountability, because it's easy to get off track and all of a sudden you find yourself a long way from your destination.

In my life, my wife provides accountability. I have software in every computer I use to block questionable content. As responsibility increases in your life, you might need to add another layer of accountability. If you really love what you're doing, keep your values in perspective. Often the actions we take to preserve our legacies or protect our jobs ironically become the very things that destroy them.

Coach Dungy knows what we would all do well to learn: the greater the power one acquires, the greater the temptation to compromise one's integrity. The secret of avoiding falling into that temptation, he says, is building a network of accountability.

In nearly every area of life, we've witnessed disasters resulting from unaccountable, influential people. Lives have been ruined, reputations have been tarnished, innocence has been shattered. In the case of Penn State, for example, we can only dream about how today would look different for those children if only one school official had taken appropriate action. I wonder how many children would have been spared if only the university's president had phoned another colleague of high character who could have spoken honestly with him. What if Paterno, throughout the years of his career, had instituted an accountability system that had brought others into this situation? Would tragedy have been averted?

There's no crisis management course for many of the problems you will face in the real world. But as Tony Dungy reminds us, integrity enables you to be courageous in the face of crises like these. When the temptation to compromise arises, when we flirt with doing the wrong thing, when the desire to protect ourselves or our careers urges us to walk a path we should avoid, the honesty of our friends calls us to our senses and protects us from disaster.

twenty-seven: Influence

Andy Andrews
New York Times Bestselling Author

I was five years old when Gail came to live with us. My parents had known her family for several years, and they had watched in consternation as the young girl had been neglected and mistreated. Her mother was battling substance abuse, which often created an unstable, even abusive environment. Having been married and divorced three times, she had opened the home to a live-in boyfriend, who carried his own set of problems. Barring an intervention or a miracle, Gail was destined for a tough life of her own.

When her mom ran away with a fifth man, Gail was left with no one to care for her. My parents jumped into action, picking her up and bringing her into our home. About ten days later, her mom returned and demanded that we release her daughter. My parents reasoned that they could provide a more stable environment, and she finally consented to let her daughter remain.

Gail became a big sister to me—she was present on my first day of kindergarten—and I watched my parents make modest, daily deposits of kindness into the bank of her life. They helped her with her homework, took her to work, and assured her that she was loved. A year and half later, Gail was a new young woman. With her high school diploma in hand, she headed off to college in pursuit of an education she might not have had otherwise.

Today, Gail is happily married to a minister with whom she has three children and two grandchildren. They reside in Illinois, where Gail has started a foundation that mentors disadvantaged girls who are in a similar position to the one she escaped. She has reconnected with her mother, who now admits her wrongdoing. Her entire family now looks to her for leadership and guidance. Gail is a trophy of grace.

If you ask her, Gail would tell you that in many ways, she still considers herself a part of our family. My parents would be quick to add that she was the daughter they never had. She lived with us at a critical crossroads, and I often wonder how different her life would be today if my parents had not intervened. We can't know for sure, but we do know that my parents' small investment made a sizable impact on the lives of more than half a dozen people. Her children bear the fingerprints of my parents' investment, as do her grandkids. My wife and I have been impacted, and we thought of Gail as we discussed adopting our children. Like a pebble in a pond, the influence continues to ripple.

Gail's story was fresh in my mind when I chose the question I would ask Andy Andrews, the bestselling author of *The Traveler's Gift* and *The Noticer*. *The New York Times* called Andy a "modern-day Will Rogers who has quietly become one of the most influential people in America." I wanted to glean his perspective on the power we all have to spark exponential influence.

KC: You are a prolific student of successful people and have read hundreds of biographies. When you think of influence, is there a story that sticks out in your mind that illustrates the powerful impact that one person can have on the world?

AA: Norman Borlaug comes to mind. Most people have never heard of him. Norman Borlaug won the Nobel Peace Prize for his work hybridizing corn and wheat for arid climates and saving two billion people from starvation on our planet. That is truly incredible, but see, by reading so many biographies and understanding the difference that we can make, I know it wasn't really Norman Borlaug who was responsible for hybridizing corn and wheat for arid climates; it was a guy named Henry Wallace.

Henry Wallace was vice president of the United States under President Franklin D. Roosevelt. Roosevelt had three vice presidents during his four terms. The second one was the former secretary of agriculture, a man named Henry Wallace. While Wallace was vice president, he used the power of his office to create a station in Mexico whose sole purpose was to hybridize corn and wheat for arid climates. Then he hired a young man named Norman Borlaug to run the operation. So it was Norman Borlaug who won the Nobel Prize, but when you think about it, it was really Henry Wallace who saved the two billion people.

Unless maybe it was George Washington Carver.

When George Washington Carver was nineteen years old and a student at Iowa State University, he had a dairy sciences professor named Wallace who on Saturday and Sunday afternoons would allow Carver to take his six-year-old boy on botanical expeditions. So it was George Washington Carver who took this little boy and put a vision in his life about plants and what they could do for humanity. It was George Washington Carver who poured into little six-year-old Henry Wallace, long before the boy ever thought about being vice president of the United States, and pointed his life in a direction.

George Washington Carver developed 266 things from the peanut that we still use today and 88 things from the sweet potato. But when you think about it, by mentoring a six-year-old boy on a few afternoons one summer, he just happened to save the lives of two billion people and counting.

Andy's story reveals a lesson we would do well to recognize. Every person on planet Earth has the power to shape futures and change lives. When George Washington Carver was just a student, he could not have known that his investment in Henry A. Wallace would shape the mind of a future vice president of the United States. And he also wouldn't have guessed that Wallace would in turn hire Norman Borlaug to run a Mexican agricultural outpost. Carver would have been flabbergasted if you'd told him that because of his seemingly small investment, billions of lives would be saved. One person with an idea, a vote, or a willingness to serve can set off a chain reaction that can literally change the world.

Influence is not exclusive to those with platform, celebrity, money, or power. Rather, it is directly related to the investments we make in others. When you tutor a child, donate to a charity, support an underprivileged family through the holidays, you are dropping a pebble in the pond of someone else's life. The ripples roll out, even if you never see where they dissipate.

When my parents picked up Gail that day, they weren't trying to change the world. They were just doing the right thing, helping a young girl who needed someone to believe in her. Gail's story, like Borlaug's, forces us to determine how we might make small deposits in others' lives right now. You might never know the scope of the impact you're having, but you can be sure that it will pay dividends.

twenty-eight:
Leading with Love

Ken Blanchard
New York Times Bestselling Author and "Chief Spiritual Officer" of
the Ken Blanchard Companies

I've had many bosses in my life, but none compares with Don. Several years ago, I was hired to work at a company where he served as CEO. When I arrived my first day, I began to hear rumors about Don. He was like a mythical creature who brightened days and quelled frustration. When his name came up in conversation, someone would inevitably shout from across the room, "Don? Aw. We love Don!" And he was loved. Deservedly.

The epitome of a relational leader, Don never forgot a name and rarely a birthday. He smiled perpetually, and, though he would not be able to get away with it today, he'd often hug his employees. Don reminded others that he believed in them, both by his comments and by the way he gave away authority. He'd lend an ear over lunch if someone was going through a tough spell, and he'd often end the conversation by praying with the person. His kindness and generosity created a fierce loyalty among his employees, such that everyone would put in extra effort or hours if needed.

In some offices, higher-ups are warned not to get too close to their employees. That wasn't Don's philosophy. He believed that leaders should value people, not the positions they fill. He invited employees into his home and into his life.

Don rarely fired anyone. Instead, he'd let people "fire themselves" by helping them realize that they weren't a good fit. When he recognized that an employee didn't belong in his current role, Don was known to help him find another job somewhere else before he let him go. A true servant leader, he always tried to make right decisions even if they weren't the most profitable.

Today, Don runs an assisted living company, and I've moved far away. But we still manage to talk often. When I have been plunged into grief, I've dialed Don's number. He doesn't hesitate to have a good cry. It's not often that employees maintain such a relationship with their bosses, especially after so much time has passed. I've found it difficult to let go of a man who knows not only how to lead but also how to love.

Ken Blanchard knows the value of leading like Don. With a PhD from Cornell University and the Grand Canyon University business school named after him, you might expect Ken to be a domineering bulldozer. He couldn't be further from that. The author or coauthor of more than thirty bestselling books, including *The One-Minute Manager* and *Leading with LUV*, he is the cofounder and "chief spiritual officer" of the Ken Blanchard Companies. I couldn't think of anyone better suited for a question on how influencers can love those they lead.

KC: How do leaders develop an authentic love for the people they are leading?

KB: At the Ken Blanchard Companies, our four ranked values are: one, ethical behavior; two, relationships; three, success; and four, learning. Why are relationships so important to us that we rank them ahead of success? Because without a commitment to building quality relationships with our people and our customers, we know we wouldn't be successful. We feel that both relationships and results are critical for the long-term survival of an organization.

There's nothing complicated about learning to love your people—it's just a matter of taking the time to get to know them on a personal level. Through the years, many businesspeople have had a traditional military attitude that says, in effect, "Don't get close to your direct reports. You can't make hard decisions if you have an emotional attachment to your people." We have found the opposite to be true. It's having that reciprocal love, trust, and caring between leadership and employees that has brought our company through some tough times. When your employees know you truly care about them, they will work hard—even make sacrifices if necessary—to help you achieve your vision.

One of the best ways for leaders to get to know each of their direct reports is to schedule regular one-on-one meetings. These meetings occur a minimum of once every two weeks and last between fifteen and thirty minutes. The meetings are scheduled by the leader, but the direct report comes up with the agenda. This gives employees an opportunity to talk to their managers about anything they wish; it's their meeting. The primary purpose of these meetings is for managers and direct reports to get to know each other as human beings. One-on-one meetings not only deepen the power of any performance review process, they also foster genuine relationships as well as a higher level of employee engagement.

Of course, not everyone is a perfect fit for every organization. What should you do if, in the process of getting to know a direct report, you begin to suspect that the person is a real mismatch for your organizational culture and values? Bring it up. Discuss your concerns and get a feel for whether or not the person is interested in a shift in thinking and behavior. If the employee does come around and this works out to be another "love connection" with the organization, all the better. But if it becomes obvious that no change is forthcoming, you may need to do what Garry Ridge, CEO of WD-40 Company, suggests: "Share that person with the competition."

Someone once asked my wife, Margie, "You have been married to Ken for almost fifty years. What do you think leadership is all about?" Margie said, "Leadership is not about love—it is love. It's loving your mission, it's loving your customers, it's loving your people, and it's loving yourself enough to get out of the way so other people can be magnificent." I couldn't agree more. Leading with love is the best way to get great results and human satisfaction at the same time.

Leaders spend a lot of time trying to gain their team's respect but not enough time developing their affections. Nourishing emotions is not easy, and employees have to be intentionally pursued. Leaders should strive to remember others' birthdays and anniversaries—as well as what they fear, crave, and are energized by. Throughout the year, they should plan retreats and outings where office talk is off limits and team members are forced to get to know one another.

Love is the disease you want to catch, and it is contagious. If you develop a loving relationship with your team, it will spread throughout the organization. As Margie Blanchard says, employees will begin to love the company and love the mission and love the work they do. Sure, it will ensure that you receive the best results from your people. But more important, it will create an environment in which your team is as excited to see you as you are to see them.

twenty-nine: Gratitude

Tim Sanders
New York Times Bestselling Author

He was given the name Benny at birth, but to me he was always Coach Polk. His razor-thin frame and bowlegged gait visually offset a mustache that would have made Tom Selleck jealous, and his thick accent betrayed his southern heritage. Coach Polk was the kind of guy you expected to see with a long piece of straw hanging out of his mouth, but that impression was misleading.

Though his words lacked velvet, Coach was a textbook motivator and brought a fiery intensity to high school basketball. Watching him develop a game plan was like receiving a lesson in detail, and he never failed to prepare his team to execute. I count the years I played basketball for Coach Polk as some of the most memorable of my life.

I remember the moment I knew Coach believed in me. My junior year of high school was my first playing varsity, which meant I was the first man off the bench in my position. We traveled to play a tournament in Norfolk, Virginia, and we'd been matched up against a highly ranked team. All week, we'd heard stories of their superstar shooting guard, and he seemed to grow in talent and size every time his name came up.

By the time the game started, our team was more than nervous. By halftime, we were down double digits. The game was threatening to slip through our fingers when Coach Polk leaned forward, peered down the bench, and barked my last name. I jumped off the bench and took a knee in front of him. With our noses nearly touching and his hand on my shoulder, he said, "Go shut that kid down."

Anyone who has played the sport of basketball knows the significance of the request. Coach Polk wouldn't have asked me to do something unless he knew I was capable of carrying it out. Emboldened, I rushed onto the court like a lightning bolt and harassed the other team's shooting guard until the buzzer sounded. When the game concluded, our team had lost, but I had won my coach's confidence.

Playing for Coach Polk was a series of big moments like those: instances in life when you learn something about yourself, your spirit lifts, and you feel part of something important. Creating times like those in players' lives was Coach's specialty, but it wasn't until I was thirty-two that I realized I'd never thanked him for his investment in me. Had I joined the ranks of the ungrateful?

With each passing year, I grow more aware of the rampant ingratitude of our world. Yet a few voices have pushed against this trend, and *New York Times* bestselling author Tim Sanders is first among them. He has championed gratitude as a key virtue for winning in business and in life. When I sat down with Tim recently, I wanted to know if gratitude is icing on life's cake or a critical ingredient of the cake itself.

KC: Gratitude seems to be a fleeting attitude in today's world. How vital is gratitude to our daily lives?

TS: Gratitude changes you as a person. I remember talking to a taxi driver just a few months ago about "have to"/"get to," something I do every morning, where I convert today's activities into opportunities instead of obligations. He told me that he was raised in an Eastern European culture, and his grandmother taught him to believe that "gratitude" is a compound word: it is the words "gracious" and "attitude" fused together. That was such an "Aha!" moment for me.

We are so much more effective in dealing with people and accomplishing things when we are gracious. I have taken a look at a lot of research; for example, if you Google "good Samaritan studies" or "good Samaritan research," you will understand that when a person has a moment of gratitude he is much more likely to cooperate and help others in need, even strangers. If we put twenty or thirty minutes every morning into just isolating who in the world is helping us and why are they doing it, we will program ourselves to start every day with a very important message: *You are not alone.*

Every morning I recount the two people who helped me the most yesterday and the person who will help me in the coming day. As I visualize them, I think of the "why." When you ask yourself, why did a good person do something to help me? you will conquer "luckitis." The answer will never be "Because he felt like it." It is always one of a couple of answers: (A) he is on a mission with me, or (B) he loves and cares about me. So the "why" behind the gratitude exercise is critical.

The value of expressing gratitude every day is that it creates positive feedback. Most of the time, when you express gratitude to someone helping you in what you are trying to do, they will tell you you deserve it. They will tell you the mission is important. They will tell you they care about you. Those are very important messages you need coming in from the outside.

> "We are so much more effective in dealing with people and accomplishing things when we are gracious."

Whenever possible, I express gratitude. I express it sometimes as formally as a note, or a call, or a conversational thank-you. There is an old saying that says that feeling gratitude but not expressing it is like wrapping up a gift and never giving it.

Tim's perspective is both refreshing and essential. I consider all the times I've lived a "have-to" life when I should have been nurturing a "get-to" mind-set. Do I have to stop by the grocery store for my wife, or do I get to serve her through running a quick errand? Do I have to trudge through my to-do list today, or do I get to pursue the work I love by achieving small goals toward greater ends? Perspective changes everything, and it means the difference between entitlement and gratitude. Offering thanks should be not an act but rather a lifestyle.

What about you? Do you view life's mundane tasks and annoyances as tasks you *must* do or things you *get to* do? How might a small shift in perspective breathe new life into your days and cultivate thanksgiving in your heart?

Shortly after I turned thirty-two, I decided to visit my parents for a week and realized I had an opportunity to reconnect with Coach Polk. I looked up the contact information for the school where he was now the athletic director and anxiously dialed the number.

A familiar baritone voice answered, "Benny Polk's office."

I paused. "Coach Polk, it's Ken Coleman."

He was pleased to hear from me. We quickly got caught up and began to reminisce. I told him I was coming to visit and planned to see him. We scheduled a time. A few weeks later, I arrived at my parents' home, eager to see Coach Polk. After everyone had finished lunch one day, I slipped away to make my appointment.

When I walked into his office, Coach embraced me as he might a familiar relative. Sitting down in opposing chairs, we laughed and recalled stories of great wins and crushing defeats. My heart warmed at the excitement he got from proudly introducing me as his former player each time a coworker stopped in. After our time concluded, he walked me to the parking lot and my face turned serious.

"Coach," I said, "I never told you how grateful I was for your investment in me, but I want to do that now. I admired you so much as a leader, and you made a real impact on my life. I can't thank you enough."

His tall frame bent a little, and his eyes filled with tears. He explained that he hadn't heard from any of my other teammates. From what I could tell, mine was the only thanks he had received. My simple extension of gratitude moved him deeply, and as I turned to get back into my car, the gruff southern man told me he loved me.

As I slowly drove back to my parents' house, I pondered how often we go through life forgetting those who've shaped our lives. Tim is right: ingratitude is like wrapping a gift but never giving it. I'd been grateful for Coach Polk's investment, but I'd never expressed it. He'd needed that gift all those years it had been collecting dust in my heart.

Most people see gratitude as an option, but we should regard it as a duty. After all, the giver needs it as much as the recipient. The day I went back to see my coach reminded me of the importance of that duty. But more important, I'd worked out my gratitude muscle and vowed never to let myself get so out of shape again.

thirty: Reciprocity

Tom Ziglar
CEO of Ziglar

Folding a navy blue sweatshirt and stuffing it into a cardboard box, I gazed around my room to determine if I'd missed anything. Moving to college was bittersweet because, even though I embraced the promise of a new adventure, I'm sentimental by nature. "It's only a four-hour drive," I consoled myself.

My eyes locked in on a shelf full of trophies and team pictures, each a fond memory and a reminder of a unique season of life. On the two shelves below rested my favorite books, including several Hardy Boys books that should be required reading for middle school boys and *Roots* by Alex Haley, which remains my favorite novel.

A slim inspirational book wedged between two larger books caught my eye. I recalled receiving it as a graduation gift, but I'd never read it. I picked up the volume, sat down to the familiar creaks of my antique childhood bed, and began to read. Page upon page was filled with quotes ranging from trite to heartwarming, but one caused me to pause:

> *You can have everything in life you want,*
> *if you will just help other people get what they want.*
> —Zig Ziglar

The words washed over me, and their simple wisdom clung to my being. This was basically the Golden Rule with a boomerang effect: we all need help at various stages in our lives, but we must first become the type of people who help others. As an old proverb reminds us, "A man who has friends must show himself friendly." I closed the book, packed the boxes into my car, and said good-bye to my parents. But Ziglar's words stayed with me.

For more than a decade, I have attempted to live out this advice. I've done pro bono work for nonprofits when I could have used that time at a paying job. I've invested in the lives of people younger than I, asking nothing in return. My wife and I have let people who needed a home live with us, and we even gave one of our cars to a seventeen-year-old girl. My 1991 Ford Taurus lacked air-conditioning, but it ran well and could have fetched a decent price had I placed an ad in the classifieds. But when I heard that the young girl needed transportation for her job, Ziglar's words returned to my mind. We gave the vehicle away and never looked back.

Throughout that time, our bills were always paid. People have taken amazing chances on me and my career. When I've needed a friend, one has always been waiting. The advice has proved true in our lives again and again.

But the quote also walks along the fine edge of manipulation. When you're ambitious, the temptation grows to leverage others who can help you in return. I often found myself doing good for others while expecting something back. My motive soured, but I rationalized that the end justified the means. Most times I fell into that trap, things didn't work out as well as I'd hoped.

In late 2011, I had the opportunity to talk with Zig Ziglar's son, Tom. Now the CEO of Ziglar, he knows his father's heart better than anyone. I wanted to ask him how to live this principle while avoiding the obvious pitfalls it presents.

KC: Your father has famously said, "You can have everything in life you want if you will just help enough other people get what they want." How do we authentically live that statement without succumbing to the temptation to manipulate others?

TZ: Reciprocation is the way the world is meant to work, but one's motives determine everything. To be authentic in this, you have to help people without any regard or concern for what you are going to get in return. People will quickly see through you, so this is very important.

Treat people with respect, listen to people, and understand the needs of others so you can help them. When you do this, not only are you helping them get what they need, you are also developing trust. I always say that people will buy from you once because they like you but they will buy from you continually if they trust you.

Helping people is much more than just giving people what they want. When I was twelve, my dad took me to a shop to pick out a bike at Christmas. There was only one salesperson, so we waited while he helped a grandmother purchase a bike for her grandson. The grandson was about six years old and was riding a bike all over the shop while his grandmother was looking at another bike.

I overheard the salesman say, "That is a great bike! Who is it for?" The lady pointed at her grandson and said, "Well, it is for my grandson over there." The salesman said, "Let's bring the boy over and see how he sits on it." As soon as the young boy sat on the bike, it was obvious the bike was too big. The salesman pointed out that the bike her grandson was riding around the shop was the same type of bike, only a smaller frame and a better fit.

The grandmother replied, "I want to buy him this bike because our neighbor has this exact one." Shaking his head, the salesman responded, "Well, ma'am, I'm sorry. This bike is too big for your grandson. I can't sleep well at night knowing your grandson might not be able to stop in time and could end up in the street or have a big accident. I can't sell you this bike."

Well, the grandmother got really mad and left. So now the salesman approached us and asked how he could help. Dad told him, "This is my son, Tom. He needs a bike, so help him pick one out." Dad knew by witnessing his interaction with the grandmother that this gentleman was trustworthy and was going to recommend the best bike for me.

The salesman knew what was best for that grandmother. His motives were to make sure that her grandson had a bike that fit him and was safe. The salesman forfeited the sale with the grandmother because he stuck to his principles. As a result, he gained my dad's trust and he got the sale with us. I have said many times, coincidence is just God's way of staying anonymous.

To really understand the thought "You can have everything in life you want if you just help enough other people get what they want," you have to know what people truly need. By building relationships and discerning their needs, you can help them based on what is best for them. You should help who you can when you can because you can.

Many times people will offer help but they don't want to. They offer their services as manipulation. We have to guard against this. Don't help people because they can help you. In fact, if you want to keep your motives pure, go find someone who can absolutely do nothing for you and help him.

Tom's words brought fresh meaning to the advice I'd read long before. The principle is not about the action—this isn't some type of karma—but rather about the motive. We help whomever we can whenever we can simply because we can. The key is maintaining a pure heart while scouting for moments, big and small, to offer ourselves. When the opportunities arise, Tom says, we must move simply because we are able.

We must resist the desire to turn Ziglar's call for generous living into opportunism, which rarely works. Society is skeptical, and people are perceptive. They can sniff out malicious motives. So do for others with the idea of receiving nothing more than the joy that comes with a good deed. Give because you have the capacity to give and someone else has a need you can meet. But, as Tom says, be prepared—because good deeds have a way of finding a person who lives generously.

This advice is a principle, not an absolute. That doesn't mean that if you are a good person, someone is going to show up and hand you a Publishers Clearinghouse check. Sometimes you will do the right thing and still get the shaft. At the same time, if you live an others-oriented life, you will often find help when you need it.

The story Tom tells is especially revealing. The bike salesman let a sale walk out the door because it was the right thing to do. He was helping the lady, though she didn't recognize it at the time. But by losing one sale, he gained another. You won't always get the sale, but you will always reap a reward. You'll live with the peace of knowing you did the right thing. When you offer yourself to others, you get a helper's high. You experience grace and reward in the act itself. Helping has a way of helping you.

So find ways to give to someone who can't give back. Offer yourself to those who have nothing to offer you. The next time a person in tattered clothes asks you for money, give it to him without judging his motives. The next time someone taps you on the shoulder to ask for help, don't be too busy. Encourage someone who has been beaten down by life's storms, and seek out moments to breathe life into those who are dying under the world's weight. In meeting the needs of others, you just might find the very thing you've been missing.

thirty-one: Womanhood

Robin McGraw
New York Times Bestselling Author and Wife of Television's
Dr. Phil McGraw

When my wife and I were struggling through our failed adoption, Stacy had a revelation. Having just been told that we weren't allowed to see the baby anymore, we returned to our hotel room in Oklahoma. I shuffled through the doorway, collapsed onto the bed, and wept. Stacy walked into the bathroom, and as she showered, I could hear her sobbing over the pitter-patter of water. Moments later she emerged and sat next to me on the bed. Rubbing my back, she said, "No matter what happens, I want to come out of this and figure out a way to help these young birth mothers who come from broken circumstances."

My red eyes looked into hers, and I admired her nobility. Whereas so many others would have been self-focused in that moment, Stacy was thinking of how to help others. Surely selflessness is one of the characteristics I love most about my wife.

When we returned home, the fire that was lit inside of Stacy seemed to grow. One day, she said, she wanted to mentor and equip birth mothers. We worked on a model together for what that might look like, but as time passed, the reality of our lives hindered us. I worked hard to provide financially for our family, and Stacy made a voluntary decision to care full-time for our three young children. We both desired to make Stacy's dream a reality—and we will—but we struggle to see how such a vision is possible for us right now.

Many women today are in similar situations. Some single mothers, for example, feel prevented from pursuing their passions because of obligations to provide for their families. I wanted to seek out a strong female voice who could speak directly to women like Stacy about reaching their full potential both inside and outside their homes.

Robin McGraw is the wife of the mental health professional and famed television host Dr. Phil McGraw. She's often spoken on his show about how seriously she takes her job of homemaker. At the same time, she's not an antiquated or oppressed woman; she is an active philanthropist, an author, and a popular speaker at events across the United States. She knows how difficult it is to pursue one's dreams while balancing the complex needs of the modern-day household. With Stacy in mind, I prepared one question for Robin McGraw.

KC: My wife has a passion for helping birth mothers who place their children for adoption and would like to work in this capacity one day. At the same time, she is proud to be a wife and mother right now. What advice would you give women like her who balance the hectic roles of wife and mother while harboring a passion to do something great outside of the home?

RM: That is a really good question, and a very important one. A lot of women I know struggle with timing and wanting to know when and how to go about doing what they love, while at the same time filling the most important role, in my opinion, of being a mother. I have always said I feel I was put on earth to be a wife and mother. From a very young age, I wanted to get married, have children, and be a stay-at-home mom, and thankfully, I was able to do that. But I never wanted that to be the only thing that defined me.

Women are very efficient multitaskers. We can do a lot, we take on a lot and, because of that, a lot is expected of us. Because we do so much and are so important to so many people, it's easy for women to feel guilty if we take away from any of those roles. Do not let that guilt get to you. You have to realize that there are no perfect women out there. We have to give ourselves a break once in a while.

I do not think it is selfish to put yourself at the top of the list and do what it is that you need to do to enrich your own life, whether it is a bath at the end of the day or a job outside the home. We shouldn't feel guilty about those things. We are better mothers and better wives and better women when we know that we have given to ourselves as we have everybody else.

Women need to identify what they need. You have to have a timeline, you have to have a plan, and you have to do it because days turn into weeks and weeks turn into months and months turn into years. If you don't have a plan, you'll likely wake up one day and realize you never did anything for yourself. I started drafting my plan early on, and my husband and boys have always been supportive of me.

When I was thirty-one, I was talking to my mother on the phone, and she said, "You know what? I am feeling kind of funny right now." Before I even could respond, she was already dead. She died of a heart attack while on the phone with me. I remember thinking that if my mother had just taken care of herself, she would still be here. She died of undiagnosed heart disease that day because she never went to the doctor and she never took care of herself.

We were very poor growing up. There were five of us children, and I never remember my mother going to the doctor. Not one time. I never remember my mother doing something for herself. She lived for her kids and my father. Partly as a result, she died at the very young age of fifty-eight from undiagnosed heart disease.

The day my mother died, I decided that I was going to take care of myself. I resolved not to perpetuate the legacy of self-neglect. I am going to take care of myself because I want to be here for my children, for my husband, and now for my grandchildren. Every time you take care of yourself, you are taking care of your child's mother and your grandchild's grandmother. I am fifty-eight now—the same age my mother was when she died—and I feel as if my life has just begun.

> "If you don't have a plan, you'll likely wake up one day and realize you never did anything for yourself."

I was touched by the way Robin spoke of her commitment to family life. Some "progressive" women today look down upon homemakers. They can't imagine why a woman would devote her life to raising children and caring for a home. I'm often confused by the condescension of these women when I consider the hard work and devotion of my wife. Stacy could have continued her career after we had children, but she determined that her primary calling was to become the CEO of our household. She's a gifted woman who works as hard as any businessperson in the United States. We agree that women who feel led to the marketplace should pursue that calling but those who choose to invest their energy and time in their families should be lauded as well.

Regardless of where a woman chooses to work, she also needs to invest in her full range of passions. And she should do so without guilt. Stacy is waiting on the right time to begin the work with birth mothers that she feels called to. And when it arrives, she may need to make sacrifices in other areas of life. We will walk that path without shame.

McGraw tells women that it's not "selfish to put yourself at the top of the list and do what it is that you need to do to enrich your own life." She adds, "I am going to take care of myself because I want to be here for my children, for my husband, and now for my grandchildren. Every time you take care of yourself, you are taking care of your child's mother and your grandchild's grandmother." Mothers, wives, homemakers, and working women shouldn't feel ashamed about taking time to invest in themselves. As McGraw points out, such actions aren't self-serving. In fact, sometimes investing in yourself is the best way to serve those you love most.

thirty-two: Health

Denise Austin
Fitness Icon and *New York Times* Bestselling Author

I'll never forget the day I received news that my friend Adam had died. Stacy and I were vacationing in Las Vegas at the Mandalay Bay Resort and Casino. We greeted the morning with reluctance, sleeping late and strolling downstairs for the breakfast buffet just before the restaurant transitioned to lunch. A couple we were traveling with sat across from us as we planned the day's agenda. My cell phone vibrated atop the table, and the name of a coworker from the IT department flashed across the screen. Thinking there must be a problem, I answered.

"Ken," he blurted out, "Adam has passed."

I asked him to clarify what he meant.

"Adam is dead."

My heart seized in my chest, and my head spun. Adam was a good friend and coworker who played on a recreational basketball team with me. As the head of event logistics, he and a few other employees had been wrapping a crate for shipment. Without warning, his eyes had rolled up in his head and he had collapsed. Our CEO, who was trained in CPR, heard screams and came running to assist. By the time he arrived, Adam was convulsing on the floor. Our CEO performed mouth-to-mouth resuscitation, pausing occasionally to spit out vomit, but neither he nor the first responders were able to resuscitate Adam. The coroner later informed us that his "widow maker" had been almost completely blocked. The infamous coronary artery had earned its name once more.

At a mere twenty-seven years old, Adam was gone, his life cut dreadfully short. How do you process the passing of someone so young due to a heart attack? I didn't know.

The day after Stacy and I returned home, I woke with a creeping paranoia. I felt a phantom chest pain when I stepped out of bed and another as I poured the coffee. Before breakfast, I called to confirm that my life insurance policy was still active. During breakfast, I called my doctor to schedule a stress test, physical examination, and EKG. After showering, I stared at my bare body in the mirror and began to take inventory of my own physical health.

When I married at twenty-three, I had been working for the governor of Virginia in a stressful, demanding job. My weight had begun to creep up. After that, I had worked around the clock for a speakers' bureau in Nashville. Sitting in a chair all day and cutting deals, I'd grown sedentary and lethargic. Less than six years later I stood before a mirror and stared at a body that was thirty-five pounds heavier. At five feet, nine inches, that's more than a little water weight. I thought of Adam, who had been about my size when he died, and decided I needed to make a change. My health was too important to neglect.

Denise Austin is a fitness icon and pioneer. She's created nearly a hundred exercise videos and DVDs that have sold more than twenty million copies, and she's starred in the longest-running fitness program in the history of television. A former member of the President's Council on Physical Fitness and Sports, Austin has been trumpeting her message for decades, inspiring people like me to make our health a priority. I figured she was the perfect person to ask about the effect health has on one's success.

KC: Most people know that health is important, yet many can't seem to squeeze exercise and proper nutrition into their busy schedules. How much more effective would we be in chasing our dreams if we were in better physical health?

DA: It makes a huge difference in the sense of energy and positive feelings, with our jobs, our relationships, our kids. I've got energy flowing because I've exercised. I've eaten well, so I've got vitamins and nutrients helping me. You could have all the money in the world, but if you don't have good health, you have nothing.

I don't think people are lazy. They just don't know how good they'd feel if they tried to improve their health. And for women, it's a little different. I'm a mom, I come from a big family with a lot of sisters, and I have a lot of girlfriends. As women, we want to take care of everybody first, and we don't prioritize our health. We're so worried about our kids and everything else that we take a backseat and then our health does, too. But for guys, I think they're just too busy sometimes. But even the president finds time to exercise. The most successful people seem to find time to exercise.

I tell people that they don't have to run a marathon. They don't even have to join a gym. Just take thirty minutes of your sixteen waking hours to devote to your body, and that's it. It could be walking or toning or yoga. It only takes half an hour. I try to convince people that it's not that difficult to improve one's health. I receive letters from people all over the country, and it took a heart attack or a cancer scare to consider improving their health. They forget that they could have prevented the crisis.

> "The most successful people seem to find time to exercise."

I don't put people down or make them feel guilty. I try to stay positive. I say, "Oh, my gosh! You'll feel so much better, I promise, if you just start with ten minutes a day of exercise and then build upon that. Just start small and gradual and make it a habit—even if it's ten minutes carved into your morning. Rather than overwhelm people, I try to give them hope that if they'll pursue better health, they'll lose weight, feel better, and be more productive."

One of the most overlooked keys to personal success is physical fitness. As people attempt to go further in life, they focus on working harder, working longer, networking better, and leading stronger. But each of those things is diminished if we inhabit an unhealthy body. Austin is right. We can't be serious about our professional life, family life, or personal life if we ignore our physical fitness.

After my conversion in front of the mirror following Adam's death, I adjusted my diet. Taking note of my calorie intake, I made junk food and sodas a fleeting memory. I increased the number of times I ate each day to increase my metabolism. I began using the gym membership that my workplace provided. The habit was difficult to form at first, but I thought of Adam with every mile I ran and every weight I lifted. Days turned into months, and I began to slim down and tone up.

I suddenly brimmed with energy. Even though my workout had replaced many hours of overtime, I was getting more done at work. As I became more disciplined in my workout, I became more efficient at the office. I discovered that some of my best thinking came when I was on the elliptical machine. Thanks to the changes I had made, I was sleeping better and feeling less stressed, more confident, and happier.

I still think of Adam from time to time—what he might be doing, what his life would look like today if he were still alive. His passing was a sorrowful reminder of life's brevity and the importance of spending it wisely. I want to properly steward every aspect of my life so long as I continue to draw breath. And whenever the clock of my life ticks its final time, I want to be proud of what I leave behind.

thirty-three: Fulfillment

Tony Robbins
New York Times Bestselling Author and Success Coach

After a famous Coleman "breakfast for dinner," I tucked my children into bed. Stacy didn't feel well, so she decided to retire early. Wired from a long day of work, I tiptoed downstairs for a guilty pleasure. Late-night television is a wilderness, but if you wander through it long enough, oases of sitcom reruns, reality shows, and Steven Seagal movies abound.

After three or four dozen channels, I noticed that *Oprah's Next Chapter* was about to start. I've secretly nurtured respect and admiration for the talk-show host over the years, and since none of my buddies were present, I selected it. I discovered that a new format had not diminished Oprah's ability to find a story, conduct a meaty interview, and stay on message: "helping others live their best life." She hooked me within minutes.

The episode featured Tony Robbins, another person who intrigues me. One of the United States' most famous motivational speakers and performance coaches, Robbins has worked with Fortune 500 companies and coached influencers including Quincy Jones, Serena Williams, and the fashion designer Donna Karan. He has been named among the "Top 200 Business Gurus" by Harvard Business School, and his books *Awaken the Giant Within* and *Unlimited Power* have been international bestsellers.

Oprah spent the day at a Tony Robbins seminar, a gathering perhaps best described as part pep rally, part business seminar, part revival. When Robbins spoke, the charged crowd could hardly remain seated. Oprah laughed, cried, and furiously took notes. When the event concluded, the daytime diva removed her shoes and walked the path all participants must: a stretch of burning coals. Talk about entertaining television.

In the second half of the show, Oprah shared some of her reflections from the seminar. Each time she made a comment, Robbins responded with a clearly rehearsed but undeniably powerful maxim. One in particular struck me: "Success without fulfillment is failure. It's not about what you get, it is about who you become." Robbins's goal isn't to help people *achieve* success but rather to *sustain* it.

I walked back upstairs when the show concluded, continuing to ruminate on Robbins's words. How do you become the person you need to be to achieve the dreams inside your head, and how do you sustain success over thirty or forty or fifty years? The only way to answer such a question, I concluded, was to ask Robbins himself.

KC: One of the toughest things about chasing one's dream is feeling as if you never hit your stride. How can dream chasers achieve their full potential and find fulfillment in life?

TR: Fulfilling your dreams and your ability to thrive in the key areas of your life can be simplified by breakthroughs—moments in time when the impossible becomes possible. If people want to thrive in any area of their lives, they have to reach a point of breakthrough where they will not settle for anything less than extraordinary. Whether they want a breakthrough in their business, intimate life, emotional well-being, health, finances, or career, there are only three areas to break through in order to experience lasting success.

One breakthrough area is your strategies. I personally live for finding strategies—those shortcuts that help people get more done in less time. What is it that gets some people to succeed while others fail, when they both seem to have equal enthusiasm or passion for the tasks at hand? Those who succeed have insights, distinctions, and strategies that allow them to achieve more quickly.

For example, take someone who was born very poor without an education and had emotional and financial challenges but found a way to be highly successful and live an inspired life. I don't believe that's luck. Luck is what you do for a day or a week; strategies are what make it consistently happen for decades.

We're not hurting for strategies. For example, there are hundreds or even thousands of strategies out there for losing weight, and frankly, most of them are proven to work—if you work them! There are fitness clubs on every street, dieticians, health coaches, training videos, audios, books, etc. Yet sixty-five percent of the United States is overweight and thirty-three percent is obese, and the number is growing. I would suggest that the problem for most people is not that they don't have a strategy—it's that they're not using a strategy that works for them or acting upon it. Why? Because they have a disempowering story.

We all have stories—a narrative we tell ourselves about why we can or cannot do or achieve something in our lives, whether we believe we can or can't—and we're usually right because our expectation controls our focus, perceptions, and the way in which we feel and act. When people succeed, it's because they have the right strategy, and they usually found it because they had a story that it was possible or they could make it happen. Often people are not losing weight because they have a simple story that says, "I'm big-boned." With that as your core belief system, you are never going to find a strategy, and even if you do, you won't follow through on it.

Your story may be true; you may have been through a horrific experience. But that's not the reason you can't have the life you want. For example, you might have had a bad breakup five years ago, but that's not the reason you haven't found the passionate and loving relationship you deserve. A disempowering story is one of the things that controls people and gets them stuck in their beliefs. Most people tell a story in a selective way so they don't have to maximize their effort toward a strategy; they're afraid they will fail. In order to get out of a story, you have to be triggered by hunger and desire; if people want something strongly enough, they will break through the story that's limiting them.

Of course, whether you have an empowering story or disempowering one is influenced most powerfully by the mental and emotional state you're in at this moment. Human beings all develop emotional patterns—moods—that are mental or emotional states that tend to filter how we look at our lives. This influences the stories we make up about who we are, what we're capable of, or what's achievable or not. The states we go into most often then become the most powerful filter of all that will determine whether we find the strategies necessary to succeed and whether we come up with a story that will empower us.

The big question then becomes, What is it that we can do to change our state of mind when we're not able to maximize our true potential? One of our greatest scientific discoveries has been that you can change your emotional mood by a radical change in your physiology.

For people who are experiencing stress at any given moment, a form of relief can be to simply change your physiology: take a couple of deep breaths. Most people only use twenty percent of their lung capacity, taking small, short breaths, but seventy percent of the body's toxins can actually be released when taking a full breath! By taking the time to fill your lungs and release, you can not only improve your health but also radically decrease the anxiety related to that moment.

There are many ways to change your physiology, and in our seminars we prove this time after time by taking people who feel depressed and helping them make a radical shift. We know intuitively that this can be changed not only by the way we move but by our breath and body temperature as well.

The second thing that affects our state is what we focus on. For example, you've been at a funeral honoring someone you cared about, and everyone is in a sad state. Afterwards someone shares an anecdote about something the person did that was extremely humorous, and suddenly everyone goes from tears to laughter. In an instant our states can be changed by what we focus on.

What's wrong is always available—but so is what's right. Whatever we focus on affects our state, and our state then affects the story we have about who we are, what life is about, what's possible, and what's not. From that story we will often determine whether or not we will maximize our capabilities and the strategies that will help us achieve what we're truly after in a sustainable way.

Learning to put yourself in a peak state consistently is one of the greatest gifts you can give yourself. It can transform your stories and give you the strategies to break through. This is a huge focus that we just don't tell people, but train people to do with their minds and bodies in an instant, on cue, so they can shift the quality of their performance. Whether it's a peak performance athlete like Serena Williams, MMA champion Jon Jones, the president of a company, a parent, or someone in prison, if we're going to shift our life, it comes down to these three fundamentals. Change your strategy, change your result. Change your story, change your life. Change your state—you change it all!

> "When people succeed, it's because they have the right strategy, and they usually found it because they had a story that it was possible or they could make it happen."

Each person gets one opportunity to live life—a single opportunity to make a difference, to live generously, to utilize his inborn talents. If you want to live fully and with sustained momentum, Robbins says, you must focus on strategy, story, and state.

As he explained each element, the truth of his insight resonated with me. But I also recognized the common denominator in each: you. When people fail to achieve momentum in life, when they stumble or underachieve, they often play the victim. Circumstances are often the first to get blamed. Then failures, others, the past, even one's genes. Such obstacles are not irrelevant and can create substantial hurdles, but none of them is insurmountable. Though Robbins admits every rule has exceptions, as a general rule *you* make the difference.

Some people were born with a silver spoon in their mouth and a trust fund lifting their bank balance, but every person can pursue his or her calling and achieve momentum in life. As Robbins reminds us, we must stop blaming and start moving. You make the difference. Live your one life well.

thirty-four: Legacy

Bob Buford
Bestselling Author and Founding Chairman of the Peter F. Drucker
Foundation for Nonprofit Management

"Chuck Norris has the heart of a small child. He keeps it in a small box."

Thus begins the satirical book *Chuck Norris Cannot Be Stopped*. But Norris is more than fodder for good jokes. He's the star of more than twenty-three motion pictures and *Walker, Texas Ranger*, the most successful Saturday-night series on CBS since *Gunsmoke*. Before becoming an entertainer, Norris was a martial arts teacher and six-time undefeated World Professional Middleweight Karate Champion. He became the first man from the Western Hemisphere to be awarded an eighth-degree black belt.

I've been fascinated by Chuck Norris ever since I watched him kick butt and take names in *Delta Force*. The film was released in 1986, yet somehow the iconic tough guy has remained relevant even at over seventy years of age. He has authored three *New York Times* bestselling books. He writes two weekly syndicated columns, makes regular cameo appearances in films, does philanthropy work, and, rumor has it, can still roundhouse-kick that smile off your face.

How does he do it?

According to a recent health and fitness column Norris penned, he's been inspired by the book *Halftime* by Bob Buford. In the book, Buford asks those entering their second phase of life, "What are five to ten core life goals that could bring significance into your life and others' lives?" Norris apparently took the question seriously.

Norris isn't the only person asking such a question. More than twelve thousand people turn fifty every day in America, and a Harvard–Met Life study shows that more than half of them want more meaning and significance in the second half of life.[1] As I read Norris's column, I was stirred by the way Buford's wisdom had motivated him. So I decided to track down the man behind Norris's—and so many others'—later-in-life success.

Bob Buford is a former cable television pioneer who cofounded Leadership Network in 1984 before becoming the founding chairman of the Peter F. Drucker Foundation for Nonprofit Management. He has penned several bestselling books, including *Halftime: Moving from Success to Significance* and *Finishing Well: The Adventure of Life Beyond Halftime*. He specializes in coaching people to live vibrantly after they turn forty.

> **KC:** The baby-boomer generation is entering retirement age in record numbers. With that in mind, what would you say to them about legacy and their ability to still make a lasting impact?
>
> **BB:** The boomers are part of a demographic wave that has in all stages of their lives changed American life, so they are going to pretty much have to make up their own rules for this season. It used to be that people lived to fifty years old, and that was it. So we don't have automatic role models in our fathers and grandfathers. They just didn't live as long.
>
> My advice to boomers or anyone in the latter phases of life can be summed up in two words: don't retire. Most people know the roles they play as school superintendent or pastor or a banker or, in my case, a cable television entrepreneur. But they aren't very clear about how their calling and strengths might transfer to something other than what they've been doing the last thirty years. We shouldn't be surprised that retirement can often bring confusion. Sure, retirement allows you to let go of those things that have been driving you crazy for the last twenty years. But you've got to retire *to* something.

Work is the psychological glue that holds the man together. It keeps us sane. With the high unemployment of the last few years, we've seen this proved true once again. People who have been out of work for a year or eighteen months experience psychological fallout, and it's not a pretty picture. People shouldn't give up their work simply because society tells them that it's time to transition into a new phase of life.

A big thing to understand is that there are three stages and seasons of life, and who you are and how you respond to different seasons is really important. The first half encompasses, on average, the first forty years. People are usually very focused on their careers during this period. Then comes halftime. This is when people generally take stock of their accomplishments and look for ways to move from success to significance. Finally, there is the second half. People can make great contributions during this stage of life, but retirees often squander much of this stage.

When I was between the ages of thirty-four and forty-two, I developed a been-there, done-that mind-set. I'd accomplished some things that built my ego, and I wanted to know what was next. I asked the classical question: is this all there is? Rather than cruise to the finish line, I decided to develop a parallel career.

When I was doing research for my book *Finishing Well*, I discovered that a lot of people did the same thing I did. They continued in their day job because it paid well and because they knew how to do it. But they began to pursue something else alongside. An example is Mike Ullman. For his whole life, he has been running retail companies. He ran duty-free stores for a while and then Macy's, and up until about three weeks ago

"Sure, retirement allows you to let go of those things that have been driving you crazy for the last twenty years. But you've got to retire *to* something."

he ran JCPenney. But at this moment, Mike is in Australia dreaming about what he's going to do next. For the last ten years or so he's been chairman of Mercy Ships, which is an organization that retrofits older ships and makes mobile hospitals out of them. Doctors volunteer their talents, and the ship becomes a floating clinic for poor people who need medical services. Mike has developed a significance career alongside his success career.

Boomers are beginning to develop margin in their lives: margins of time, margins of money, and so on. They have a choice: they can use these margins to store up for a retirement stage where they drop out of the work force, sleep late, and play hundreds of rounds of golf, or they can engage their strengths and passions in new ways.

Solomon says in Ecclesiastes 3 that there is a season for everything. A season to dance and laugh and mourn. A season to build up and a season to tear down. As one considers legacy, it's critical that we develop a clear mission for the second half of life. This will move us from success to significance as we finish out our final season on earth and move on to even better things.

Though I'm only thirty-eight, I can't imagine myself retiring. I'm energized each morning I wake and direct my mental and physical energy into my work. While I can't predict what life will look and feel like at seventy-five, I can't picture myself bailing on everything I've worked toward to play shuffleboard on cruise ships. I may not desire to push quite as hard and fast as I am now, but I don't want to stop working altogether.

Perhaps you're nearing retirement age and see things differently. You've grown weary of the nine-to-five grind, and you'd relish some time for yourself. I'd encourage you to confront Buford's question: "What are five to ten core life goals that could bring significance into your life and others' lives?" The answer might not be your current job, but it might not be daiquiris on the beach either. Write down a plan for how you want to engage your strengths and passions in the new phase of life you're approaching.

If you've got several years left before you can leave your current job, consider Buford's advice of developing a new career path alongside your current one. Let your day job fund the development and launch of your dream job. It may never become your primary source of income, but it will bring fulfillment to your life in ways your day job doesn't or can't.

I believe God has created every person on planet Earth with a purpose. And He's equipped you with talents to achieve that purpose regardless of your life stage. No matter what phase you're in, if you can find a way to do what you love, you'll strain for a compelling reason to never quit it completely.

thirty-five: Passing the Torch

Dan Cathy
President and COO of Chick-fil-A

With less than forty seconds remaining in Super Bowl XLII, Eli Manning's fingers gripped the football. His team, the New York Giants, trailed the New England Patriots by four. Only thirteen yards separated his team from the goal line and a likely win. The stadium audience held its breath, and time slowed to a near stop as Eli released the ball and connected with wide receiver Plaxico Burress. Giants fans erupted, the team having essentially secured its place as professional football's world champion.

Following the game, sports media focused their reports on several angles. Some cast Eli Manning as a David who had slain the Goliath from New England. Others honed in on the final seconds, declaring it one of the greatest Super Bowl finishes of all time. But I craved another story, one that transcended that particular game and instead focused on the rich heritage from which the winning quarterback hailed.

Eli Manning's father, Archie, is a former NFL quarterback himself and a member of the College Football Hall of Fame. Eli's brother, Peyton, was also a championship quarterback for the Indianapolis Colts. As I considered the legacy of the Manning family, I wondered how two men who had grown up in the wealthy home of a professional athlete ended up known more as workhorses than prima donnas. The "rich kid" stereotype is prevalent today and, in my experience, for good reason. Children who grow up with silver spoons in their mouths and get two of everything they want often mature into thankless, entitled adults. But the Manning brothers' reputation centers on their strong work ethic, kind demeanor, and strong character.

Digging, I found a wealth of material detailing the family's synergy and the uncommon parenting the two brothers had received. Archie and their mother, Olivia, had never missed a football game or school function. But they had purposefully sat at the top of the bleachers with smiles on their faces rather than on the sidelines berating their children's coaches for more playing time. The father, whose middle-aged faced is now accented by laugh lines, often speaks of how much he loves his children. The words seem as effortless as breathing.

Archie deserves almost as much credit, it would appear, for Eli's and Peyton's success as the sons themselves. As one sports writer commented, "Peyton Manning is as much an extension of his father and his family as a man's hand is of his arm. They are as connected as pipeline."[1] The same could surely be said of Eli as well.

As a father of two boys, I wondered how parents can successfully create such a legacy with their children. What about in the business world? How does one pass the torch to the next generation of organizational leadership?

To track down an answer, I connected with Dan Cathy. He is the president and COO of Chick-fil-A, one of the United States' most successful and beloved fast-food restaurant chains. The company was founded by his father, Truett, more than 50 years ago. But under the leadership of Dan and his brother, Bubba, who serves as senior vice president, the organization has swollen to more than 1,600 stores across the country and generates more than $4 billion in annual sales.

Chick-fil-A is known for focusing as much on people as on chicken. Its award-winning customer service transforms first-time patrons into lifetime fans, and several publications have named it one of America's best places to work. The company has thrived under Dan's leadership while maintaining all the trademark style of his father. One has to wonder what the president of this organization has learned about Manning-style torch passing. I decided to ask him.

KC: Your father, Chick-fil-A founder Truett Cathy, is now more than ninety years old. What have you learned from him about passing the torch of leadership from one generation to another?

DC: There are many lessons I have learned from Dad. Probably one of my favorites is that if you follow your passions in life, you will never have to work again. In his life and in work, Dad is a very, very passionate person. He derives tremendous joy and fulfillment not only from his work but also the things he does in his personal time. In fact, it is really quite difficult to distinguish personal time from his work because they are so rolled up together. Dad taught me that when you love what you do, when you are passionate about what you do, when you care deeply about the reasons that you are doing things, then you can sustain joy and a positive outlook for many years. It becomes innate within a person. When someone is working to raise up new leadership, he needs to make sure to pass on his passion rather than just hand over a position.

Also, you want to pass along the DNA you've worked hard to construct. Chick-fil-A's corporate purpose, for example, is to glorify God by being faithful stewards of all that is trusted to us and have a positive impact on all we come in contact with. That statement resonates very deeply with customers, who understand that we are here to acknowledge the Lord in all our ways. It also gives our employees great joy and fulfillment because they know we are being good stewards of what God has entrusted to our care in this lifetime.

But more than that, it is Dad's heartbeat for our organization. It is what makes us unique and special among restaurant businesses. We see our restaurants as places of restoration. We want our restaurants to be places that bring about not only physical restoration but also emotional and spiritual restoration in the lives of the millions of people who may eat with us in a given month. So Dad indeed did well to pass along the torch of his passion and a strong corporate DNA to me and the entire Chick-fil-A team.

Leaders often don't like to talk about passing the torch, but Dan seems quite comfortable with it. Perhaps the topic generates anxiety for some because it forces us to deal with our own mortality. Have you ever wondered why there are so few legacy stories on the cover of *Forbes*? Many companies enter a roller coaster of ups and downs after the CEO passes, but why? Perhaps we don't believe that anyone else can do as good a job as we can, or maybe we're afraid that someone else will do a better job than we did. Or is it because power and influence are intoxicating and people simply can't let go of their end of the torch? I suspect that many organizations have been sacrificed on the altars of insecurity and pride.

According to Dan, passing the torch means transmitting both passion and purpose to the next generation. That ensures that we will empower, rather than enable, those who follow in our tracks. Dan's father was known for being a passionate businessman, and somehow that leached into his sons' souls. When people, especially kids, see passion, they are attracted to it. It rubs off on them. We must not be afraid to let our fervor out.

Passion cannot be taught; it must be caught. People need to taste it and brush up against it. They need the scent of passion to fill their nostrils. The Manning boys saw their father compete on a high level, and they caught a whiff of his enthusiasm. Similarly, when employees see leaders who are passionate about their jobs, the passion often grips them too.

But raw excitement is useless unless it has a meaningful outlet. That is where purpose comes in. Just as the Mannings' passions were grounded in strong character, so the Cathys have been grounded in Chick-fil-A's corporate purpose statement. The statement makes the quick-service restaurant unique among its competitors, and their passionate employees have become the catalyst for exponential growth. Dan shares what Eli illustrated for me that Super Bowl night in 2008: if leaders find a way to pass on passion and purpose, they'll hand the next generation a winning combination.

thirty-six: Reinvention

Jimmy Carter
39th President of the United States of America

As a child, I faced few events with as much anticipation as Friday nights. As the week concluded, I coveted two days of freedom from scholastic endeavors and time with friends. Around five in the afternoon on Fridays, my mom and dad would wrangle my brother and me into the family car. I would struggle to sit still as we made our way to a wonder of wonders for a young boy: Blockbuster Video.

Walking through the door of the small store on Mercury Boulevard in Hampton, Virginia, was akin to entering an amusement park. Only a turnstile and the smell of hot dogs were lacking. A chipper salesperson in a royal blue vest would greet us, and my brother and I would wander the aisles, looking for the movie of our choice. Should we snatch a comedy? Try to convince our parents to let us rent a scarier film? Or should we forgo a movie altogether and opt instead for a video game?

For me and countless other children, Blockbuster was more than a video store; it was a symbol of endless entertainment. The retailer played an undeniable role in my childhood, introducing me to such great movies as *Top Gun* and *Hoosiers*. One of my favorite childhood memories is curling up with my family and watching *Moonstruck*, starring Cher and Nicolas Cage. We rolled with laughter, trying not to knock the popcorn out of the bowl. We still trade quotes from that film at family gatherings.

Blockbuster Video stores have gone the way of the brachiosaurus. With the cadence of a drippy faucet, the famed video franchises have been transformed into dry cleaners and cafés. Despite the chain's positive image among consumers, the rise of the digital age doomed Blockbuster's model. A little start-up by the name of Netflix came along with a promise that the movies you desired would never be out of stock. And it would even save you the drive by delivering them to your doorstep. Netflix and other media providers began harnessing technology to deliver content. Former customers like myself began wondering how all the soon-to-be-unemployed Blockbuster employees planned to spend their free days.

David Kahn owned forty-five Blockbuster franchises across the Southeast with five hundred employees, worth more than $15 million. In 2002, at the age of forty-nine, he, too, saw the writing on the wall. He was faced with a choice to attempt to ride out the storm until retirement or cut his losses and start over. He elected for the latter. "[Kahn] was in jeopardy of losing his financial security, his self-respect, his professional life," *CNN Money* recounts. "He would have to reinvent himself—or the world would do it for him."[1]

Kahn looked at his talents and determined that he didn't just know how to rent videos; his expertise was in growing franchises. Then he looked at market trends and saw a burgeoning desire for frozen yogurt. He secured a $300,000 government loan using his house as collateral and opened Yogurt Mountain on September 10, 2009. Nearly forty stores now exist, and he is partly credited for the yogurt fad that has swept the Southeast and much of the United States.[2]

David Kahn is a living testament that reinvention is possible at any stage of life, as is Jimmy Carter, the thirty-ninth president of the United States. Carter was elected on November 2, 1976, and two months later he walked hand in hand with his wife, Rosalynn, down Pennsylvania Avenue to their new home. He was the people's candidate, a populist president from the small town of Plains, Georgia. Historians consider Carter's presidency a misadventure despite his significant accomplishments, including the Camp David Accords, the establishment of diplomatic relations with China, and the SALT II treaty with the Soviet Union.

When Carter left office in January 1981, he could have retired to a vacation home somewhere and collected hefty speaker's fees. He instead chose to "pull a Kahn" and reinvent himself.

The president founded a nonprofit, the Carter Center, for the purposes of international conflict resolution and the alleviation of human suffering. He has since worked tirelessly to advance human rights and "wage peace" around the world. He is the author of more than two dozen books, volunteers one week a year with Habitat for Humanity, and serves as distinguished professor at Emory University in Atlanta, Georgia. Because of his postpresidential work, Carter was awarded the Nobel Peace Prize in 2002, "for his decades of untiring effort to find peaceful solutions to international conflicts, to advance democracy and human rights, and to promote economic and social development."[3]

When I spoke with President Carter recently, I decided to ask him one question on reinvention.

KC: Mr. President, one of the things I admire most about you is how you reinvented yourself after you left office. We have a record number of baby boomers who are entering retirement, and yet their lives can still be fulfilled and very effective. Talk to us about how we can continue forward and reinvent ourselves in a new season.

JC: I wrote a book about this particular subject a number of years ago called *The Virtues of Aging*. And I realized that a lot of people in our country retire in their forties or fifties, and they have twenty-five or thirty years ahead of them. What are they going to do with that time?

Sometimes we have a very discouraging experience in our lives; for example, I wanted to be a president for a second term and wasn't reelected. You have to make a decision about what you are going to do when you have a plan that is aborted or terminated, perhaps through no fault of your own.

You just have to look at your own talent and ability and decide where you can spend the rest of your life, your daily existence, in the most productive, enjoyable, adventurous, unpredictable, and gratifying way.

One thing that I realized was that God gives every one of us adequate talent, ability, education, or wealth to conform to God's will. Sometimes when we don't have all of the education or intelligence that we think we need, we have to accept what God gives us. We have to decide how to accommodate changing times in life—and all of us are confronted with changing times—but cling to unchanging principles, to the principles of basic moral values that apply to anyone, whether they are religious or not.

We must always ask, What does the next chapter in life look like? That is true even for those who have retired. As we age, we often slow down or, worse, shut down. We should instead be searching for new areas of achievement, fresh horizons, and bold second-phase goals.

By the time the second phase of life arrives, most of us have amassed plenty of disappointments. In Carter's case, he wasn't reelected. But the president reminds us that we can respond to disappointments with retreat or reinvention. "You have to make a decision about what you are going to do when you have a plan that is aborted or terminated, perhaps through no fault of your own," he says.

But this isn't just a golden-years lesson; it's a tutorial for any age. Reinvention is apropos for the thirty-something who got a degree in finance to please his father but feels his passions and gifts leading him down another career path. It's germane to the middle-aged working mom who was recently laid off and needs to find another way to support her family. As both Carter and Kahn illustrate, the ability to change with life creates the possibility that the next day may be the best one yet.

Final Challenge

NEVER STOP ASKING

My first infant breaths were taken in Point Pleasant, West Virginia, a river town where men wore hand-tooled boots and everyone knew everyone else. People there would rather hunt than eat, but because they could hunt, they always had a good meal. More than a dozen foothills watch over the population of fewer than five thousand working-class citizens, many of them coal miners. In 1774, Virginia militiamen famously defeated Shawnee Chief Cornstalk at the Battle of Point Pleasant, and a proud spirit lingers more than 225 years later.

Our town was a great place to raise a family. The turn-of-the-century-era downtown oozed Americana where salt-of-the-earth residents came to conduct their business. Tucker Mayes was our big-shot car dealer, but he was lucky to have forty cars sitting on his lot. Ironworkers like Eddie Van Matre walked into the bank to deposit their weekly paycheck. And presiding over it all was our mayor, the aptly named Jimmy Joe Wedge.

Our family's apartment was a few minutes outside of downtown, on the second floor above Lieving Plumbing and Heating. Before I was born, Ken and Barbara Coleman had lived there for a year or so, attempting to break into the community as outsiders who had moved from Tennessee and weathering the Ken and Barbie jokes that flowed freely from new acquaintances.

Giving birth to me was intense, and hours into the process Mom's body quit on her. The newest nurse in the room had fainted and was lying on the floor when her veteran coworker, Jan Hindy, decided to take matters into her own hands. Climbing atop my mom's weary body, she pressed the baby bump forward as the doctor pulled on my head with forceps. To this day, I always arrive late and still love a big entrance.

Even as a toddler, I possessed an intense imagination and curiosity. My mother never needed a playpen. She could place me on a blanket as a child and didn't need to watch my every move. So long as I had a toy or two, I'd dream up my own entertainment for hours, never leaving my blanket wonderland. For all its good qualities, a town like Point Pleasant didn't exactly foster such characteristics. We didn't have a science museum or a petting zoo. But curiosity sprouted from me as if a seed had been planted in my innermost parts at conception.

My mom likes to tell stories about how I would respond when I was being disciplined. When I was caught hitting my brother or talking back to my parents, I would attempt to delay my punishment by repeatedly pleading with my mother or father. When it was clear that a reprimand was imminent, I'd raise a chubby index finger and give my final plea: "Wait. Just let me tell you one question."

My parents would hold back laughter as a younger version of me rattled out a tear-soaked inquisition. Perhaps my life's calling was apparent far earlier than I realized.

The stereotype of a child asking "Why?" is more than a stereotype. Most kids are inquisitive by nature. Elementary school students tend to ask more questions than middle school students. They also tend to ask more than high school students.[1]

As researchers at the University of Michigan observed, "Examining conversational exchanges, and in particular children's reactions to the different types of information they get from adults in response to their own requests, confirms that young children are motivated to actively seek explanations. . . . When preschoolers ask 'why' questions, they're not merely trying to prolong conversation, they're trying to get to the bottom of things."[2]

Children are more than twice as likely to re-ask their question if they aren't given a clear answer, and when they do get an explanation, they are more than four times as likely to reply with a follow-up inquiry.[3]

Unfortunately, this impulse "to get to the bottom of things" often fades like a new shirt in its first washing. Most adults accept the world around them—from their career choices to their values and beliefs—as fate. At some point during adolescence, and without the slightest protest, many of us fall asleep as inquisitive children and wake as adults submitted to the hand that life has dealt.

Perhaps we decide that we're too busy for curiosity and discovery. Or perhaps we come to believe that asking questions won't bear any fruit. We begin to see life as a treasure chest filled with answers but guarded by a daunting padlock. If only we would recognize that questions are the keys that unlock life's greatest and most helpful answers.

I was not surprised recently to learn that most successful leaders are also tenacious questioners. When the veteran journalist Warren Berger studied the world's leading innovators, he discovered that they tended to be masters of the art and science of asking questions. He observed, "They have a knack for looking at the world around them—at the existing reality that everyone else usually just accepts—and asking: What if we did this? Or tried that?"[4]

How much better would our lives be, how much more fulfilling, if we developed a habit of inquiry? If we switched off our mind's autopilot and instead raised its antennae?

Recognizing the need to ask questions is much easier than the asking itself. In an age of media, one might get the impression that interviews are easy. As we drink our morning coffee or unwind after a long day at work, seasoned interviewers such as Bob Costas, Charlie Rose, Matt

Lauer, and Barbara Walters enter our living rooms and execute their jobs with ease. But when we attempt to ask tough questions of the influential people in our own lives—our husbands or wives, bosses, best friends, or neighbors—the words sink deep into our throats. After a few opportunities pass us by, we throw up our hands and move on.

How can you develop the habit of inquiry? And how can you make sure that when you finally get the words out, they matter? The answer is surprisingly simple: know the question you want to ask, and then find someone who can answer it.

ASK THE RIGHT QUESTION

A good interviewer asks questions with the audience in mind. If you don't know the audience, you can't craft the right question. For most people, they are the audience. If we don't know ourselves, the right question will be beyond our grasp.

As Leo Tolstoy once said:

> We have measured the earth, the stars, and the depths of the seas; we have discovered riverbeds and mountains on the moon. We have built clever machines, and every day we discover something new. . . . But something, some most important thing, is missing, and we do not know exactly what. We feel bad because we know lots of unnecessary things but do not know the most important—ourselves.[5]

Once you know yourself—your strengths, your passions, your sweet spot—you'll recognize the answers you don't know but need to know.

Additionally, the right question requires imagination. We must wonder what could be and how one might get there. How can this be done better? What could I do to solve this problem? How can I impact this person? We get stuck in the present only when we forget about the future.

ASK THE RIGHT PERSON

Once you have a question in mind, you have to find the right person to ask. If you ask the wrong person, you'll get the wrong answer. You don't want to ask a physics professor about U.S. history. The right question asked of the wrong person becomes the wrong question.

The persons you ask should be *knowledgeable.* They should understand the thing you are going to be asking. If it is a religious question, consider asking a minister. If it is a leadership question, think about asking a CEO.

The persons you ask should be *credible.* Knowledge is not the same as wisdom, and you want to ask your question of people who are wise—that is, they aren't only experts who have studied or researched the matter, but they've lived it.

The persons you ask should be *truthful.* The right answer does you no good if people won't give it to you. You not only need people with understanding and experience but people with the guts to tell you the truth.

ACT ON THE ANSWER

Everyone needs the discipline to ask the right question, the discernment to ask the right person, and the determination to do something about it. The last step is the most important of all. An answer is only as useful as the listener's willingness to act on it. In the preceding pages, you've encountered statements that spoke to you. They were cool water to your thirsty soul. You feel the urge, the impulse to act. An answer you've been searching for materialized on the page. That leaves you with my final question: What are you going to do about it?

Henry David Thoreau once said, "Most men lead lives of quiet desperation and go to the grave with the song still in them." As I survey the landscape of my own community and people in my network of influence, I see the wisdom of that statement affirmed. How many walk through life resigning themselves to their current reality? I believe most people live in "quiet desperation" because they've stopped asking questions. They've quieted the inquisitive child that once echoed from within.

I've started gathering my children around me each night and saying something such as "Kids, you can ask me anything you'd like. You can ask me about the moon, about God, about what makes you mad—anything. What do you want to ask?" I refuse to let the fire of curiosity flicker out, so I'm nurturing the habit of inquiry in their lives early on. They need to know that you can't act on an answer you don't have and you'll never get the answer until you ask the question.

I'm grateful that I've held on to my childhood curiosity. More than three decades after my family said good-bye to our second-floor apartment in Point Pleasant, my heart continues to pound with the same request to "let me tell you one question." As I've learned, questions blow the hush off the quiet places, they uncover valuable wisdom for every stage of life. Questions are keys that unlock life's most important answers.

As you move from discovery to legacy in your own life, I'd leave you with one final challenge: never stop asking. Keep pressing forward with tenacious curiosity. Life's greatest answers are waiting to be had if you are willing to seek them out. From my earliest memories until now, I've never stopped asking.

And I never will.

Notes

Introduction: Why Ask Questions?

1. Betsy Rothstein, "Couric on Palin: 'She Was Done with Me,'" October 6, 2011, www.mediabistro.com/fishbowldc/couric-on-palin-she-was-done-with -me_b52662#more-52662.
2. James Reston Jr., "Frost, Nixon, and Me," *Smithsonian*, January 2009, www .smithsonianmag.com/history-archaeology/Presence-Frost-Nixon.html.

Chapter 5: Opportunity

1. Laura Evenson, "A Crash Course in Cringely/How a Techno Nerd Is Triumphing as a TV Star," *San Francisco Chronicle*, November 9, 1998, www.sfgate .com/cgi-bin/article.cgi?f=/c/a/1998/11/09/DD71932.DTL.

Chapter 10: Hard Work

1. Chauncey DeVega, "When Stupid People Don't Know That They Are Stupid: Glenn Beck's Restoring Honor Rally and the Dunning-Kruger Effect," September 2, 2010, http://blogs.alternet.org/speakeasy/2010/09/02/when -stupid-people-dont-know-that-they-are-stupid-glenn-becks-restoring-honor -rally-and-the-dunning-kruger-effect/.

Chapter 17: Obstacles

1. Clay Risen, "The Lightning Rod," *The Atlantic*, November 2008, www.the atlantic.com/magazine/archive/2008/11/the-lightning-rod/7058/.
2. Ibid.

Chapter 22: Forgiveness

1. St. James Church, a family ministry, 2010, *http://saintjameschurch.com/media -podcasts-a-more/video-.*

Chapter 23: Redemption

1. Andrew Carroll, *War Letters: Extraordinary Correspondence from American Wars*, p. 106. New York, NY, Scribner, 2001
2. Susan Schmidt and Jeffrey A. Birnbaum, "Tribal Money Linked to GOP Fundraising," *The Washington Post*, December 26, 2004, www.washingtonpost .com/wp-dyn/articles/A26015–2004Dec25.html.
3. Alan Feuer, "For Ex-Lobbyist Abramoff, a Multimedia Effort at Redemption," *The New York Times*, November 12, 2011, www.nytimes.com/2011/11 /13/us/jack-abramoff-making-a-multimedia-effort-at-redemption.html?page wanted=all.

Chapter 34: Legacy

1. "What Is Halftime?," www.halftime.org/what-is-halftime/.

Chapter 35: Passing the Torch

1. Quoted in John Underwood and Archie Manning, *Manning* (New York: HarperEntertainment, 2001), 13.

Chapter 36: Reinvention

1. Douglas Alden Warshaw, "Pulling Off the Ultimate Career Makeover," June 21, 2011, http://management.fortune.cnn.com/2011/06/21/pulling-off-the -ultimate-career-makeover/; "Once Block-busted, Now Yogurt King," June 29, 2011, http://money.cnn.com/galleries/2011/pf/1106/gallery.career_reinven tion_stories.fortune/2.html.
2. "Once Block-busted, Now Yogurt King," June 29, 2011, http://money.cnn.com /galleries/2011/pf/1106/gallery.career_reinvention_stories.fortune/2.html.
3. "The Nobel Peace Prize 2002: Jimmy Carter," www.nobelprize.org/nobel _prizes/peace/laureates/2002/.

Final Challenge: Never Stop Asking

1. Po Bronson and Ashley Merryman, "The Creativity Crisis," *Newsweek*, July 10, 2001, www.thedailybeast.com/newsweek/2010/07/10/the-creativity-crisis .html.
2. Brandy N. Frazier, Susan A. Gelman, and Henry M. Wellman, "Preschoolers' Search for Explanatory Information Within Adult-Child Conversation," *Child Development* 80, no. 6 (November—December 2009), 1592–1611.
3. Ibid.

4. http://amorebeautifulquestion.com/about/; see also Warren Berger, *Glimmer: How Design Can Transform Your Life, and Maybe Even Your World* (New York: Penguin, 2009).

5. Leo Tolstoy, trans. Peter Sekirin, *Wise Thoughts for Every Day: On God, Love, the Human Spirit, and Living the Good Life* (New York: Arcade Publishing, 2011).

Find your dream job.

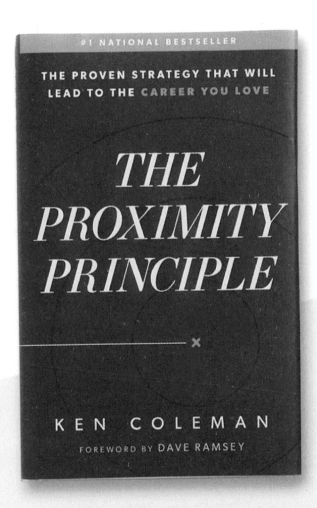

Calling all job hunters! If you're not happy with your career, you're not alone. Over 70% of Americans are unhappy with their jobs. *The Proximity Principle*, by career coach Ken Coleman, is the proven strategy that will lead you to the career you love. Learn who you need to know and where you need to be in order to find amazing new opportunities.

kencoleman.com

DISCOVER YOUR
PURPOSE
with **AMERICA'S CAREER COACH**

Check out *The Ken Coleman Show* on your favorite
platform to have your career questions answered.